W9-AEB-018

Praise for *Inclusion in Action*

"This book is a useful resource for all educational teams who plan to modify instructional curriculum or students with disabilities. Eredics provides practical ideas and ready-to-use templates for making modifications that enable students to be full members and participants in their general education classrooms. This book embodies values and pedagogy, but even more practical resources teachers can really use." —**Jennifer A. Kurth, Ph.D.,** University of Kansas

"Inclusion in Action is an extremely practical resource that all teachers will find valuable. It is an easy to understand text that provides accurate information about inclusive education. And it is full of resources that can be immediately accessed. This book is a must for all teachers who want to provide inclusive education in their classrooms." —**Kathy Wahl,** Director, Inclusion Collaborative, Santa Clara County Office of Education

"[Nicole Eredics'] international perspective and years of experience with her blog and podcasts have provided her with unique insights to the issues that teachers face within the classroom setting." —**Kathleen G. Winterman, Ed.D.,** Associate Professor and Program Director of the Special Education Program at Xavier University

"Inclusion in Action is the comprehensive handbook schools need to create meaningful inclusive school communities. It makes the case for inclusive practice and provides K-12 educators and administrators a detailed roadmap for getting there."—**Torrie Dunlap, CPLP,** Chief Executive Officer, Kids Included Together

"In clear and engaging prose, Nicole Eredics not only outlines the case for inclusion in education, but also offers helpful examples from her own teaching experience, along with sound practical strategies that educators can easily adapt for their own use. Essential reading for everyone involved in student learning." —**John Draper,** Founder of Together We Rock!

"Inclusion in Action is primed to be a game changer for educators with how they deliver special education services in inclusive classrooms. Simple, straightforward, and immediately relevant strategies for any teacher to implement, Inclusion in Action is an instant classic that will ultimately facilitate comprehensive systems change in the United States and beyond." —**Tim Villegas, CAS,** Founder and Editor-in-Chief of Think Inclusive

"I often hear educators ask 'how' to do inclusion. This book is the 'how' they've been searching for. Every educator should have this book in their mailbox!" —**Sandra Assimotos McElwee,** Author of *Who's the Slow Learner? A Chronicle of Inclusion and Exclusion*

"This should be a required book for all teachers, especially general education teachers! Nicole has put together a book that provides the essential elements for making inclusion a reality for all students. Few books on inclusive education are written specifically with the general education teacher in mind. Yet, they are the ones who will lead the way forward so that all students, regardless of their abilities or disabilities are educated together." —**Susan Marks, J.D., Ph.D., BCBA-D,** Professor of Special Education at Northern Arizona University

"Wow! What an excellent resource for general education teachers. This book is a comprehensive guide to what inclusion is and how to insure you can create an inclusive classroom for all students. I will be sure to share this book with teachers looking for new ideas to include their students." —**Brenda Giourmetakis, M.Ed.,** Supervisor of Inclusive Learning at Edmonton Public Schools

"This book provides a great foundation for educators or parents to understand the inclusion movement for students with more complex needs. Nicole provides a plethora of resources grounded in work samples for curriculum modifications to help bridge the gap for students with targeted academic needs." —**Lisa Dieker, Ph.D.,** University of Central Florida

"The title of this new book delivers on its promise – 'practical' strategies. If you are looking for lots of examples of how to include and modify for students who are working below grade level, this book is for you!" —**Anne Beninghof,** Consultant and Author, www.ideasforeducators.com

"Inclusion in Action: Practical Strategies to Modify Your Curriculum offers a practical and comprehensive approach to increasing inclusive practice across grades, disciplines and school communities. Nicole's strategies and insights are clear and attainable, and hers is a resource beneficial to all educators." —**Lisa Friedman**, Disability Inclusion Expert and Author of the Removing the Stumbling Block blog

"Nicole Eredics' book is needed more now than ever before to not only address the difficulty of including students with disabilities in the Gen. classroom, but also to show schools how to make the process work with efficacy. Nicole addresses topics for promoting inclusion through building a strong foundation for inclusive school culture to addressing positive classroom management, and collaboration between teachers, specialists, paraprofessionals, parents, and volunteers and inclusive school spaces. She leaves no stone unturned. While her coverage of the components that foster an inclusive environment is thorough, possibly her best gift to the reader is her clear explanation and examples of curriculum modifications. Inclusion in Action: Practical Strategies to Modify Your Curriculum includes hundreds of tips that are practical and easily implemented as well as forms and handouts that support the inclusive process." —**Susan Fitzell, M.Ed., CSP,** Author, Educational Consultant, and Professional Speaker

"All staff, administrators, general and special education teachers, and paraeducators can easily find themselves utilizing this book to help reach students they may not know how to otherwise connect with." —**Renay H. Marquez,** Co-Founder of ParaEducate

"The most helpful section of [Inclusion in Action] is the 40 practical strategies for curriculum modification. [Each strategy is] explained in a step-by-step manner along with specific examples showing how the strategies work. All teachers should find [these] strategies . . . doable and workable in most classrooms." —**Carolyn Coil, Ed.D.,** Educational Consultant and Author

Inclusion in Action

Inclusion in Action:

Practical Strategies to Modify Your Curriculum

by

Nicole Eredics
Mentone, CA

·P A U L·H·
BROOKES
PUBLISHING Co.®

Baltimore • London • Sydney

Paul H. Brookes Publishing Co.
Post Office Box 10624
Baltimore, Maryland 21285-0624
USA

www.brookespublishing.com

Copyright © 2018 by Paul H. Brookes Publishing Co., Inc.
All rights reserved.

"Paul H. Brookes Publishing Co." is a registered trademark of
Paul H. Brookes Publishing Co., Inc.

Typeset by Absolute Service, Inc., Towson, Maryland.
Manufactured in the United States of America by Sheridan Books, Inc., Chelsea, Michigan.

Case studies are real people or composites based on the author's experiences. Real names, likeness, and identifying details are used by permission.

Purchasers of *Inclusion in Action: Practical Strategies to Modify Your Curriculum* are granted permission to download, print, and photocopy the blank forms in Appendix B for professional or educational purposes. The forms may not be reproduced to generate revenue for any program or individual. *Unauthorized use beyond this privilege is prosecutable under federal law.* You will see the copyright protection notice at the bottom of each photocopiable page.

Library of Congress Cataloging-in-Publication Data

Names: Eredics, Nicole, author.
Title: Inclusion in action : practical strategies to modify your curriculum /
  by Nicole Eredics.
Description: Baltimore : Paul H. Brookes Publishing Co., [2018] | Includes
  bibliographical references and index.
Identifiers: LCCN 2017044892 (print) | ISBN 9781681252247 (pbk.) | ISBN 9781681252865 (epub) |
  ISBN 9781681252872 (pdf)
Subjects: LCSH: Inclusive education—Curricula—United States. | Curriculum
  change—United States.
Classification: LCC LC1201 .E74 2018 | DDC 371.9/0460973—dc23
LC record available at https://lccn.loc.gov/2017044892

British Library Cataloguing in Publication data are available from the British Library.

2022   2021   2020   2019
10   9   8   7   6   5   4   3   2

Contents

About the Forms ix

About the Author. xi

Acknowledgments xiii

Introduction xv

    The Struggle to Include. xv

    What Needs to Change? xvi

    Bridging the Gap With This Book xvii

I. Including All Students 1

    1. Preparing for Inclusion. 3

        Moving From Segregation to Inclusion 4

        Core Beliefs of Inclusive Education 6

        The Benefits of Inclusive Education. 10

        Conclusion 12

    2. Supporting Inclusion Schoolwide. 13

        The Role of School Leadership and Staff. 13

        School Culture 16

        School Community 19

        School Spaces. 20

        Conclusion 21

3. Supporting Inclusion in the Classroom 23

    The Inclusive Classroom Team: Building a Network of Support 23

    Creating an Inclusive Classroom Culture.. 29

    Conclusion 35

4. Making Curriculum Accessible Through Instructional
   Strategies and Accommodations..37

    Ways to Make Classroom Instruction Inclusive 39

    Conclusion 44

5. Making Curriculum Achievable Through Modifications.. 45

    What Are Curriculum Modifications? 47

    Why Modify? 48

    How Are Curriculum Modifications Made?.. 50

    Conclusion 52

II. Modifying Curriculum for Students Who Work Below Grade Level 55

6. Research-Based Curriculum Modifications for Inclusion......................................57

    Modifications: Different Ways to Make the Same Curriculum Achievable 57

    Maintaining High Standards While Modifying Curriculum 58

    Instructional Strategies That Modify Curriculum...59

    How to Use the Strategies 62

    Conclusion.. 62

7. The Strategies 63

    Who Benefits From Use of These Strategies?... 63

    How to Use This Chapter.. 66

    Strategies for Knowledge Retrieval 68

    Strategies for Comprehension.. 107

    Strategies for Analysis 132

    Strategies for Knowledge Utilization 146

Appendix A: Helpful Resources 155

Appendix B: Helpful Forms... 159

References 177

Index 183

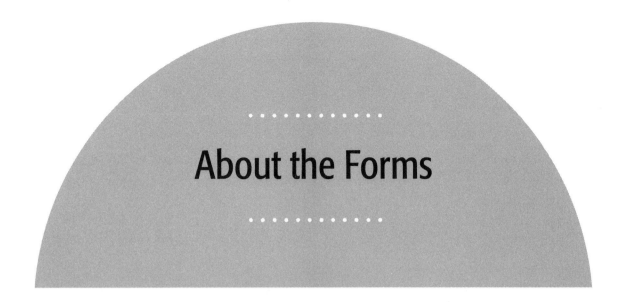

About the Forms

Purchasers of this book may download, print, and/or photocopy the blank forms for professional or educational use. These blank forms are included with the print book and are also available at www.brookespublishing.com/eredics/materials for both print and e-book buyers.

About the Author

Nicole Eredics, B.Ed., Mentone, CA

Nicole Eredics is an educator who advocates for the inclusion of students with disabilities in the general education classroom. She draws upon her years of experience as a full inclusion teacher to write, speak, and consult on the topic of inclusive education to various local and national organizations. Nicole uses her unique insight and knowledge to provide practical strategies for fully including and instructing students of all abilities in the classroom.

Nicole's advocacy work also includes managing a highly successful blog, *The Inclusive Class,* which has been a reputable resource on the topic of inclusion for families and schools since 2011. Through the blog, Nicole disseminates information about inclusion, which includes more than 100 episodes of *The Inclusive Class* podcast, dozens of articles about inclusive education, numerous webinars, and an online introductory course to inclusion. For more information please visit www.theinclusiveclass.com.

Nicole is a Canadian who traded the snow for sun and lives in Southern California with her husband, kids, and a Vizsla.

Acknowledgments

I am incredibly thankful for the opportunity I had to work as an inclusive classroom teacher in British Columbia, Canada. It is through my students and their families, colleagues, and administrators that I truly learned how to teach students with and without disabilities in the general education classroom. Through them, I also learned the numerous benefits of inclusive school systems. I saw firsthand that successful inclusion *can* and *does* happen. Most important, I realized that we need inclusive schools in order to properly prepare our students to live in the real world.

My most heartfelt appreciation also goes to my husband, Peter Eredics. The lessons I learned would have never made it on paper without you. Your own experiences and achievements were inspiration for making me think that writing a book was possible. Your love, support, and patience helped make it happen. Thank you for being with me every step of the way. I am so deeply grateful.

Much gratitude and adoration for my children, Joshua Eredics and Kristen Eredics, who always choose to be kind, compassionate, and inclusive even when their mom isn't looking. You were my motivation to keep writing about the ease and importance of including others.

My deepest thanks to Doreen Unrau, Karen Moynihan, Tasha Mahalm, and Terri Mauro who also helped me bring this book to life. You planted the seed, cheered me on, listened to my concerns, provided feedback, and gave me invaluable advice. I am also grateful to Bob and Beth Friesen and Jim and Susan Eredics for their ongoing encouragement.

Sincerest thanks to Genna Young, Max Irons, Olivia Irons, as well as Joshua and Kristen, who were part of the workforce I needed to illustrate my ideas. Much appreciation to Julie Farrell and her son Jesse, Beth Foraker and her son Patrick, Sheryl Zellis and her son Chaim, Renee Laporte, and Nathan Devlin for providing the photos in this book and showing us what an inclusive world looks like.

Finally, I would like to give a huge thanks to Paul H. Brookes Publishing Co. for publishing this book. The talented and knowledgeable staff at Brookes brought out the best in each paragraph and page I wrote.

I couldn't have done it without you all!

Introduction

Do you have students in your class who work well below grade level? Are you wondering how to include and support students with significant cognitive disabilities in your classroom? Are you relying on busywork to keep your struggling learners occupied while you teach a class lesson? You aren't alone. It is rare that every student in a classroom is competently working at grade level. Teachers can feel overwhelmed, undertrained, and unable to support students who require additional support, not to mention a modified curriculum. In fact, you might even be wondering why students who work below grade level are in general education classrooms in the first place.

THE STRUGGLE TO INCLUDE

In the United States, students whose needs are so great that they require modified programs are typically known as *students who receive special education services* or *students with disabilities*. These terms stem from an eligibility requirement that students must fall into one of 13 disability categories to qualify for special education. Thus, much of the literature and research in the United States around special education and, subsequently, inclusive education uses the term *students with disabilities*. Historically, students with disabilities were educated in self-contained classrooms separate from their peers. Segregated settings were deemed more appropriate for students with disabilities because they provided smaller class sizes and developmentally appropriate curriculum and fostered self-esteem (Heller, Holtzman, & Messick, 1982). Yet, years of research and practice have proved that these students do not have to be removed from the general education classroom to receive their modified instruction. In the general education classroom, students with and without disabilities can flourish with a curriculum rich in academic content and social opportunities. In fact, "no studies conducted since the late 1970s have shown an academic advantage for students with intellectual and other developmental disabilities educated in separate settings" (Falvey, 2004, pp. 9–10). Since the 1970s, improved attitudes and higher expectations have led to the development of federal legislation to provide guidance in educating students with disabilities. The Individuals with Disabilities Education Act (IDEA), reauthorized in 2004 (PL 108-446), mandated that students with disabilities have access to the general education curriculum in the least restrictive educational setting.

However, educators are still clearly challenged by the practice of inclusion. In 2016 it was reported by the National Center for Education Statistics that in the 2012–2013 school year, only 61% of students with disabilities spent 80% or more of their time in general education classrooms. Of the different types of students with disabilities, students who have speech and language impairments spent most of their time (87%) in general education classrooms. Meanwhile, only 16% of students with intellectual disabilities and 13% of students with multiple disabilities had the same opportunity (National Center for Education Statistics, 2016). Furthermore, Kurth, Morningstar, and Kozleski found that there has been "little progress in reducing restrictive setting placement options" (2014, p. 20) for students with certain significant disabilities. These data speak volumes. Teachers in general education classrooms are successfully making the accommodations necessary to include most students with disabilities. However, it appears that there is a systematic failure to include students with intellectual and multiple disabilities. The continued use of self-contained special education classrooms for instruction of these children flies in the face of federal legislation and research-based educational best practices.

WHAT NEEDS TO CHANGE?

The path to inclusion requires a collaborative, team-based approach to educating students with disabilities, along with the knowledge of best educational practices for engaging all learners in core curriculum content. Calls for a more integrated approach to special education have been made for years. In 2002, the President's Commission on Excellence in Special Education formally supported the idea that students who receive special education services are to be regarded as general education students first (Blanton, Pugach, & Florian, 2011). Likewise, the National Research Council stated that schools must "integrate general and special education service and apply high-quality instruction based on evidence-based practices to assure and achieve better academic outcomes for all students" (Donovan & Cross, 2002). Yet, special education teachers have long taken responsibility for the education of students with disabilities in general education classrooms, with a heavy reliance on the special educator to provide academic support and programming for students who require a modified curriculum. Despite recommendations, studies show that preservice training on teaching students with disabilities remains limited. In one particular study, researchers sought to determine what type of explicit training in teaching students with disabilities that teachers in the United States received in their teacher preparation courses. In analyzing the number of university courses dedicated to teaching students with disabilities in inclusive settings, researchers found that "many university teacher preparation programs in elementary education are allocating minimal coursework to issues related to disabilities and may not be adequately preparing their graduates for entry into today's inclusive schools" (Allday, Neilsen-Gatti, & Hudson, 2013). According to Cameron and Cook, "general educators reported taking 1.5 courses on average in which inclusion or special education content was a major focus, as opposed to approximately 11 courses for special educators" (2007, p. 360). In a report to the United States Government Accountability Office in July 2009, researchers found that teacher preparation programs varied greatly in their course requirements, with just over half requiring teachers to take a course related to teaching students with disabilities. In a 2011 paper prepared for the American Association of Colleges for Teacher Education and the National Center for Learning Disabilities, researchers Blanton and colleagues observed that less than one third of teacher preparation programs required field experiences with students who have disabilities.

In other words, many classroom teachers spend most of their preservice training learning how to teach typically developing students, with little attention given to working with students who have significant intellectual, social, emotional, and physical disabilities.

It's little wonder that inclusive education often receives a lukewarm reception at best by classroom teachers. It can be overwhelming and challenging for teachers with limited training and experience to include students with disabilities in the classroom, particularly in the content areas of the curriculum. Lack of teacher training can have a tremendous impact on teacher attitudes and behaviors. Sharma and Nuttal (2015) studied the attitudes of preservice teachers toward inclusive education before and after a university course that focused on the benefits of inclusion as well as strategies for inclusion. Results showed that the preservice teachers' attitudes toward educating students with disabilities in the general education classroom improved dramatically after the course.

To successfully provide inclusive educational experiences, teachers need to know that it is the legal and social right of all learners in the United States. Both general and special education teachers need to have the skills and knowledge to provide an inclusive educational environment. Teachers also need to know that inclusion benefits all students, and that years of research tell us inclusion is the best educational practice for students with disabilities. In addition, teachers must know the structures and systems that support inclusion. Staff training, accessible spaces, appropriate learning materials, and a responsive curriculum are all essential elements of inclusive education. Finally, and most important, both general and special education teachers need practical strategies to facilitate inclusion in the curriculum. General educators and special educators must be able to deliver a modified program not just to students with mild to moderate disabilities but also to those students with severe intellectual and physical challenges. Educators must have the skills and knowledge to provide learning accommodations as well as modified content by making substitutions, alterations, and changes to the curriculum that are educationally appropriate and inclusive.

BRIDGING THE GAP WITH THIS BOOK

Whether you are new to the concept of inclusion or in need of more ideas to modify curriculum, this book is a resource for today's classroom. It can help bridge the gap between special education and general education for students who are working below grade level and require a modified program to access the curriculum and achieve academic success. The goal of *Inclusion in Action: Practical Strategies to Modify Your Curriculum* is to give practical, accurate information about inclusive education and provide concrete strategies for curriculum modification. Section I, Including All Students, introduces you to the basics of inclusion and the path to providing all students access to the general education curriculum, with information on how to create an optimal educational environment that supports students with disabilities without segregating them from their peers. Specifically, Section I provides a framework for understanding inclusive education by looking at supports at the school, classroom, and curriculum level. In Section II, Modifying Curriculum for Students Who Work Below Grade Level, you'll learn how to put the fundamentals of inclusion into practice with a collection of 40 proven strategies to modify the curriculum for students who work below grade level, so they can participate in core subject areas such as math, English language arts, science, and social studies. Most of these strategies are adaptable for students of various ages and are applicable to a range of core content areas. Each modification strategy also contains extension ideas. Visual examples of student activities are provided to help you understand how each strategy works.

Please note that the strategies provided in this book do not constitute a systematic, sequenced program for curriculum modification, nor do they reflect the full range of assistive technology currently available for use in working with students with significant intellectual disabilities. Rather, these strategies are "light-tech," paper-and-pencil modifications. They are designed to be flexible enough to be adapted for use anytime, anywhere, across a range of subjects, ages, and ability levels. It is my hope that as you review the strategies, you will be inspired to find ways to use them creatively with the particular students and subjects you teach. If you wish to explore more structured curriculum modification programs, see Appendix A, which provides a list of numerous online, print, and audiovisual resources to create and supplement modified curriculum for students. In addition, Appendix B includes blank printable templates for immediate use in applying the strategies in this book within your classroom.

This book is not meant to be a textbook on inclusion, but rather a professional resource that combines the principles of high-quality, effective instruction with the knowledge and information you need to be an inclusive educator. In addition to providing numerous tips and strategies, I also share advice and stories directly from the field, based on my years of experience working with students on modified programs in general education, in the hopes of sharing insight into how inclusive education can actually work.

Note that throughout this book, I use people-first language when referring to students who have a disability. People-first language is a commonly used framework that provides guidance in speaking to and speaking about people with disabilities. It is based on the belief that we are, first and foremost, people with distinct interests, abilities, challenges, and dislikes. People-first language recognizes that certain terms and phrases that have been historically used to describe people with disabilities are dehumanizing and offensive. The Arc notes, "People-First Language is an objective way of acknowledging, communicating, and reporting on disabilities. It eliminates generalizations and stereotypes, by focusing on the person rather than the disability" (2016). Some examples of people-first language include using the term *student with autism* rather than *autistic student,* or *students with disabilities* instead of *disabled students.* Most schools and organizations have adopted a people-first language policy that provides appropriate terminology for staff and communities. (See Chapter 2 for more on language and an inclusive school culture.) If you are in doubt of what term a person with disabilities would prefer you to use, you can just ask him or her.

I want to thank you for taking the time to read this book. I hope you can add some of the suggested strategies for including all students and modifying curriculum to your repertoire of teaching skills. They don't all have to be used at once. Start small and try at least one new strategy. If needed, tweak or change these strategies so that they fit the needs of your classroom. Make it work to reach, teach, engage, and include our least included learners!

SECTION I

....

Including All Students

CHAPTER 1

· · · · · · · · · · · · ·

Preparing for Inclusion

General education teachers who lack the training and skills required to successfully teach students with disabilities can feel anxious and unprepared for inclusive environments. Their reliance on special education teachers, paraprofessionals, and resource rooms can displace a student who requires alternative education programs, leading to an inequality in educational experiences and opportunities for children with disabilities. This chapter equips all teachers with the foundational knowledge they need to prepare for working in an inclusive environment. Knowing the fundamental concepts of inclusion can guide educators in creating meaningful and equitable educational opportunities for all students. Teachers who are prepared for inclusion feel confident that they are providing students with an education proven to have substantial benefits for all types of learners. They understand that inclusion is an approach to education that supports students in areas such as intellectual, social, emotional, and physical development. Finally, they know the difference between environments that are truly inclusive and those that do more harm than good. Having a strong understanding of inclusion must preclude its implementation and practice.

TIPS FROM AN INCLUSIVE EDUCATOR:

Committing to Inclusion

While I was working toward my education degree during the late 1980s in British Columbia, Canada, exciting changes were taking place in the provincial school system. It was undergoing a major shift in its philosophy, purpose, and structure. Using the latest educational research, schools were restructuring for the purpose of inclusive education. The goal was to provide students with an appropriate, meaningful education in their neighborhood schools and classrooms. Supports and specialized services for individual students were to be delivered in the context of the general education classroom. School staff was training in methods and strategies for the instruction of all learners. Resources in the form of assistive technology and learning materials were distributed throughout the schools; paraprofessionals were hired to help. Parents and communities were consulted. An inclusive school system was taking shape.

Fortunately, my preservice training was responsive to the changes in the school system. We were introduced to methods of instruction for all students. We took classes in learning disabilities and special education. We also had a series of practicums in which we spent time teaching in classrooms that were inclusive. By the time I graduated with my teaching degree, I had an understanding of inclusion. Most important, I had skills and strategies that I was eager and ready to use in an inclusive classroom. It's my hope to share this knowledge with new and veteran educators who are preparing to work in inclusive classrooms. Here are some tips for teachers who are new to inclusive education:

Learn—Learn as much about the practice of inclusive education as you can. Understand what inclusion is and what it is not. There are many myths about inclusion that can sabotage an inclusive classroom. For example, people who are not familiar with inclusive education may worry that the academic progress of typically developing students will be negatively affected in an inclusive classroom. However, research shows that inclusion does not affect the academic and social development of typically developing students. (See additional discussion of this point throughout this chapter.)

Collect—Gather information, ideas, and strategies that will help you establish an inclusive environment. Bookmark web sites, search Pinterest boards, keep notes, and take photos of materials and/or environments that are inclusive. (Be sure to check out the list of resources in Appendix A at the back of this book!)

Connect—Find others who are familiar with inclusive education. Twitter and Facebook have numerous groups of educators and parents who are interested in discussing inclusive practice. Arrange to observe a teacher who works in an inclusive classroom. Share resources with one another, such as inclusive lesson plans, classroom management tips, and helpful apps. Creating a network of support will help you feel confident as you develop your skills as an inclusive educator.

This chapter begins with a brief look at the historical origins of inclusion and why this movement still struggles to gain nationwide traction in the United States. Next, I discuss the relevance of inclusion in today's world, why it is necessary for our schools, and how it benefits both typically and nontypically developing students. Finally, I will name other teaching philosophies, such as mainstreaming and integration, which can mask themselves as inclusion but are not.

MOVING FROM SEGREGATION TO INCLUSION

Historically, public school education in the United States did not involve children with any kind of disability. People believed that students with intellectual, physical, or developmental delays were better educated in separate settings. Worse, those settings often included an institutionalized or residential placement where education was a low priority. If there was an opportunity for education, it was largely based on a child's medical diagnosis. Broad assumptions were made about a child's ability level and potential accomplishments. Public education split into two separate education systems where students with disabilities did not mix with students in general education classes (Reynolds & Birch, 1982).

In the 1960s, a man by the name of Burton Blatt started a movement to humanize and deinstitutionalize people with intellectual disabilities (IDs) in the United States. Osgood (2005) tells us that Blatt published one of the 1960s' most significant critiques in the field of special education. In his work, *Some Persistently Recurring Assumptions Concerning the Mentally Subnormal,* Blatt looked at some of the myths surrounding children with intellectual disabilities. After publication of Blatt's work, questions from advocates and researchers began to arise about the quality of instruction and the benefits of educating certain students in separate classes or schools.

By the mid-1960s, a cascade of services for special education began to evolve through the early work of Elizabeth Deno (1970) and Maynard Reynolds (1962). Described as a continuum of services for students with disabilities, the cascade included multiple types of educational settings, each more or less segregated than the one before. Through the 1970s, schools used the cascade model to guide the acceptance and placement of students with disabilities. Such placements included resource rooms, part-time special classes, and full-time special classes. Interestingly, Reynolds later became critical of the use of the cascade model. He felt that students in special education were better off receiving a continuum of supports within the least restrictive environment of the general education classroom. Other prominent special education supporters followed suit in this thinking. In 1968, Dr. Lloyd Dunn criticized the segregation of students with disabilities in his paper "Special Education for the Mildly Retarded—Is Much of It Justifiable?" He asserted that many students were misidentified as having special needs due to poor socioeconomic circumstances. He believed that some disabilities stemmed from low-quality home and school life. He further suggested that students were marginalized because of their level of functioning. Dunn (1968) confessed:

> In my view, much of our past and present practices are morally and educationally wrong. . . .
> Let us stop being pressured into continuing and expanding a special education program that
> we know now to be undesirable for many of the children we are dedicated to serve. (p. 5)

The realization that students with disabilities have a right to the same education and experiences as their typically developing peers continued to gain momentum. Instructional models began to change and support the inclusion of students with disabilities in general education. Madeline Will, who was Assistant Secretary of the U.S. Department of Education, wrote a landmark paper in 1986. In her report, more commonly known as the "Regular Education Initiative," she called for a cohesive, uniform education system that was more inclusive. Notable research continued to make educators think about special education services, such as Steve Taylor's 1988 work, "Caught in the Continuum: A Critical Analysis of the Principle of the Least Restrictive Environment," in which he wondered why students with disabilities needed to "earn" their way into a general education classroom.

Through a series of legislations and reauthorizations, the Individuals with Disabilities Education Improvement Act (IDEA) of 2004 (PL 108-446) was created to reflect current beliefs about special education. This law governs the education of individuals with disabilities in the United States, ensuring that every student has the right to a free appropriate public education (FAPE). IDEA 2004 does not use the word *inclusion,* but it does state a preference for having students with disabilities placed in the "least restrictive environment." Specifically, IDEA 2004 states that children are to be educated in the regular education environment to the maximum extent possible with appropriate aids and supports. The types of appropriate aids and supports a student might receive include assistive technology, access to occupational therapy, and a modified curriculum. If the nature of the child's disability is severe enough that supplementary aids and services provided by the school and/or teacher cannot help the child achieve satisfactory progress, then another educational placement will be considered (U.S. Department of Education, 2016). Ensuring that students receive adequate supplementary aids and services is the obvious key to creating more inclusive opportunities for our students, particularly those with intellectual and multiple disabilities who are, by far, least likely to be fully included in general education classrooms.

An international organization called the United Nations Educational, Scientific, and Cultural Organization (UNESCO) exists to support quality, inclusive education around the globe. In 1994, UNESCO stated that inclusive schools were the most effective way to counter discriminatory approaches and attitudes toward students (Loreman, Forlin, Chambers, Sharma, & Deppeler, 2014, p. 4). Since then, international legislation has developed to combat the practice of exclusion and segregation in schools. Countries such as Canada, Denmark, and New Zealand have well-developed policies that support inclusive education.

According to UNESCO, barriers to inclusion can include curriculum that is not designed to meet the needs of diverse learners, teachers who are not sufficiently trained to work with students with disabilities, and inadequate resources (e.g., lack of qualified staff, inappropriate learning materials, minimal supports). Perhaps the biggest barriers to inclusion, however, are ingrained attitudes and beliefs that marginalize students with disabilities. In an article titled "Barriers to Inclusive Education," UNESCO stated, "The greatest barriers to inclusion are caused by society, not by particular medical impairments" (2016). These attitudes might include low expectations about the student's ability to learn, negative stereotypes about people with disabilities, and the tendency to blame a child's learning difficulties on his or her differences rather than on a failing of the educational system. The next section discusses the beliefs that are the building blocks for successful inclusion.

CORE BELIEFS OF INCLUSIVE EDUCATION

Inclusive education is a philosophy with a set of associated attitudes and approaches to educating all children. It is based on the belief that students of all abilities have the right to an education that is meaningful, appropriate, and equivalent to that of their peers. Experts and researchers agree that every student is valued, respected, and supported in an inclusive classroom and that inclusion is a collaborative, whole-school effort. According to Grima-Farrell, Bain, and McDonagh, "Inclusive education represents a whole-school concern and works to align special education with general education in a manner that most effectively and efficiently imparts quality education to all students" (2011, p. 118). In an overview of inclusive education, Loreman and colleagues (2014) stated the following:

> Hall (1996, cited in Florian, 2005) notes that inclusion means, "Full membership of an age-appropriate class in your local school doing the same lessons as other pupils and it mattering if you are not there. Plus you have friends who spend time with you outside of school." (p. 6)

For inclusive education to prevail and become the standard in U.S. schools, society needs to have and maintain several core beliefs that are the foundations for inclusive education. Those core beliefs center around the student, the school, and our vision for students' future beyond school. Let's look at each foundational belief a little more closely.

Beliefs About Students

Traditionally, American schools have all too often regarded students with disabilities as incompetent based on their performance on intelligence and adaptive behavior tests. Proponents of inclusive education believe that all students of all competency levels are welcome in general education classrooms. They know that every child is capable of learning. Rather than use medical labels or emphasize the student's specific disability, inclusive educators teach all students based on their unique strengths and intellectual, social, emotional, and physical needs. They focus on the individual child and his or her potential rather than differences or deficits. Supporters of inclusion uphold the need to "presume competence" in students with disabilities. Jorgensen, McSheehan, and Sonnenmeier (2007) found that when teachers presume competence, students with disabilities are more frequently engaged in appropriate grade-level curriculum. Furthermore, research on the academic outcomes of students with disabilities drives home the importance of providing high-quality curriculum with appropriate supports and rigorous learning expectations (Cole, Waldron, & Majd, 2004; Theoharis & Causton-Theoharis, 2010). Inclusive educators believe that no one can predict the outcomes of the interaction between students and teachers. The best approach, according to Biklen and Burke (2006), is for teachers to choose the most optimistic outlook possible and assume that their students are competent and capable of learning.

Figure 1.1. Jesse, a third grader, shows his modified spelling test. (Contributed by Julie Farrell.)

Inclusive educators also believe in valuing student differences and supporting their learning needs to the greatest extent possible. Teachers, paraprofessionals, and special educators have supports in place to enhance the child's ability to learn. For example, if a student has difficulty with printing his or her responses to a reading comprehension question, the teacher or assistant can scribe for the student. In other words, the student verbally gives the teacher his or her response and the teacher writes the response for the student. Some may wonder if this is fair practice. For people who are unfamiliar with inclusion, it may appear that the student who is receiving help from the teacher has an extra advantage over his or her peers. However, consider this scenario. If a child has difficulty seeing the work that is displayed on the whiteboard at the front of the class, we do not hesitate to recommend vision screening for eyeglasses. Once the student has eyeglasses, is he now at an advantage over his peers with perfect vision? No. Instead, the student now has the same opportunity as his classmates to see the whiteboard and learn the material. For this reason, inclusive educators believe that students must have the supports, accommodations, and modifications they need in order to learn the same materials as the rest of the class. In Figure 1.1, Jesse shows his modified spelling test. Jesse works with the same spelling words as his peers, yet the list is modified for his ability level. Instead of writing the entire word, Jesse completed each word by inserting the missing letters shown in the left column of the page.

Beliefs About School

For inclusion to be successful, it is important that we understand how inclusive education fits within schools and what a school's responsibility is in providing an equitable education to all children. Schools are known to have all sorts of programs to support student interests and needs. There are reading programs, buddy programs, and anti-bullying programs. Inclusion programs differ by nature from other school programs and clubs; there are no set criteria for inclusion. Inclusion isn't just another program to be implemented; it is a school-wide approach to providing every student access to a rich and varied educational experience. Inclusive education does not have a timetable. Nor does it happen in a classroom down the hall—there is no such thing as an "inclusion classroom." We don't *do* inclusion. Rather, we *live* inclusion, adopting the attitude that students are fully participating, valued members of the school community in everything we do. Inclusive education occurs in all settings, and students are included to the greatest extent possible in every aspect of the school day, from academic classes to assemblies, clubs, music programs, and science fairs. If a child needs extra support, appropriate services are brought to the student in the classroom.

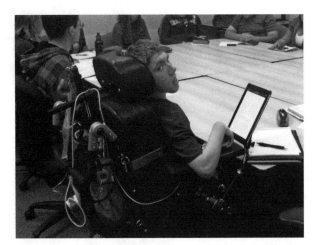

Figure 1.2. Nathan uses an assistive device to help him participate in a class discussion. (Contributed by Renee Laporte.)

Figure 1.2 shows a student using an assistive communication device, which enables his participation in class. Also, if needed, students can use alternate spaces where interventions and intensive, direct support can occur. Above all, "The practice of inclusion is not necessarily synonymous with full integration in regular classrooms, and goes beyond placement to include meaningful participation and the promotion of interaction with others" (Province of British Columbia, 2016).

Without knowledge and understanding, inclusion can be easily confused with two other educational practices that are used to bring students with disabilities into general education classes: *mainstreaming* and *integration*. However, both of these practices are significantly different from inclusion in their purpose and outcome for students and for teachers.

The first practice, mainstreaming, gives a student with disabilities access to the general education classroom, provided that he or she can meet certain benchmarks in the curriculum. For example, if a student who is placed in a special education classroom can demonstrate age-appropriate behavior and grade-level skills, he or she may be eligible to spend part of the day in a corresponding general education classroom. In essence, the student has to fit into the existing structures and systems of the classroom. When he or she does not, the student returns to the special education classroom. In this situation, the special education teacher still retains responsibility for the overall education of the student.

The second practice, integration, is one step closer to inclusion, but there are still differences in the student's level of participation and sense of belonging in integration. Students with disabilities are placed in general education classes when the classroom can be adapted to meet some of the child's needs. For example, the classroom might need to be physically accessible, have the support of a paraprofessional, and/or offer assistive technology. The teacher includes the child in some lessons, depending on the child's ability to comprehend the grade-level material. If not, the child works on an alternative program with the paraprofessional, either in or out of the classroom. A student who is integrated has more opportunities to interact with his or her peers than a child who is mainstreamed. With the level of participation in class activities varying throughout the day, however, it can be challenging for the student who is integrated to develop relationships.

Figure 1.3 provides a visual of the differences among exclusion, mainstreaming,

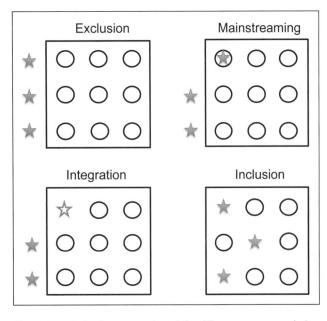

Figure 1.3. A visual representation of the differences among exclusion, separation, integration, and inclusion.

integration, and inclusion. In this image, stars represent students with disabilities, whereas circles represent students with typically developing abilities. The box in the top left-hand corner depicts an educational environment in which the exclusion of students with disabilities prevails. When a school environment supports mainstreaming, as represented in the box in the upper right corner, we can see that the student with disabilities must be able to fit into the existing structures of the general education class. The box in the bottom left-hand corner is an example of integration. In this setting, the student with disabilities, represented by the outline of a star, is in the classroom but may not be a fully participating member. Finally, in an inclusive setting, all students of varying abilities are welcomed into the classroom where they share the same educational experiences; no single student is set conspicuously apart or stands out.

According to Marsha Forest and Jack Pearpoint (1995), pioneers in the inclusive education movement, there is only one criterion required for being included: *breathing*. Unlike in mainstreaming and integration, there are no predetermined criteria for being a member of an inclusive class. Inclusive classrooms do not expect the student with disabilities to fit into their structure. Instead, inclusive schools provide a classroom structure suitable for the student. For example, seating areas, lighting, learning materials, behavior interventions, and assignments can be adapted or modified to support student participation. The school assesses the unique needs of each student to determine the most appropriate educational setting in the least restrictive environment. A student's placement in an inclusive school is fluid, with the student moving through educational settings that best meet his or her needs at the time.

Beliefs About Life Beyond School

All students have a right to become contributing members of society. In fact, according to the publication *Why We Still Need Public Schools: Public Education for the Common Good* (Center on Education Policy, 2007), there are several purposes for public education, and equity in opportunity is one of them. We include all students in our classrooms because all students have the right to reach their full potential and achieve personal success. When we exclude an entire group of children based on their differences and disabilities, we immediately limit their development as well as ours. Our number and types of interactions with one another are reduced, as well as opportunities to learn from one another. Countless people with disabilities make significant contributions to our society and live rich, fulfilling lives. They are people involved in every sphere, from art, music, film, and literature to mathematics, science, business, and agriculture. As an example, many people who have lived with a disability are well known for their accomplishments: Temple Grandin, Helen Keller, Stephen Hawking, John Nash, Vincent Van Gogh, Albert Einstein, and others. Yet, these individuals should not be seen as isolated success stories or exceptions to the rule, or seen only as sources of great inspiration. The National Collaborative on Workforce and Disability (2017) cautions against using stereotypes and hero worship to describe or identify people with disabilities. This practice can lead to unfair standards and expectations of behavior. Rather than being seen as exceptional for being active members of society, people with disabilities should be treated just like all other individuals—each treated as merely human and a regular contributing member of the community who has adapted to his or her own set of challenges (National Collaborative on Workforce and Disability, 2017).

When it comes to educating children with disabilities, it is important to recognize that exclusion and separate treatment in school do not reflect the world around us. Every day, families, communities, and jobs demonstrate inclusive behavior in life outside of school. For example, parents adapt and accommodate for the needs of their children to facilitate full participation in the family unit. We buy strollers for our babies who are not yet able to walk. We prepare food with the allergies and tastes of our offspring in mind. In our communities, we speak a little louder for those who are hard of hearing. We stand in line next to one another at the grocery store, share the road, have equal access to public venues, and hold the door open for a stranger carrying bags of groceries. We do so because supporting and including others has benefits for everyone. It only makes sense that public education aligns itself with the values and supports that exist in our society.

THE BENEFITS OF INCLUSIVE EDUCATION

If you are new to the idea of inclusion, you might wonder if inclusive education will be disruptive to your class. You might be concerned that that there will be an increase in behavior that is inappropriate. Or, you might be already aware that inclusive education is a huge benefit to students with disabilities, but you may worry about how your typically developing students will adjust. The following sections provide an overview of the proven benefits that inclusive education has for *all* students.

Emotional Benefits

Inclusive classrooms are places that provide a sense of belonging. They accept students with various skill levels, are responsive to student needs, and focus on student strengths. Students with disabilities are not marginalized or separated from their peers. In his work, *Toward a Psychology of Being,* renowned American psychologist Abraham Maslow (1962) described a hierarchy of human needs, beginning with lower level, basic needs such as food and water, and moving up to higher level needs such as love and a sense of belonging. He theorized that humans move through an ascending order of needs, with each level of need having to be met before the person can move on to the next. Maslow believed that achieving these needs made people feel motivated and helped them realize potential and fulfillment, with the needs for love and belonging being critical for human development. Alternatively, Maslow believed that when our needs are not met, we fail to maximize our potential as humans. We feel ostracized, secluded, and alone. Our behaviors and interactions with others become stilted and underdeveloped. Segregation and exclusion create feelings of isolation, thus minimizing the desire to better oneself.

Of the needs Maslow identified, a sense of belonging is particularly relevant to educational research. Research makes it clear that one of the decisive factors in educational success is the feeling of belonging, and a sense of belonging has long been thought to be an important component of education. Carol Goodenow proposed that a sense of belonging at school reflects "the extent to which students feel personally accepted, respected, included, and supported by others in the school social environment" (1993, p. 80). In a review of educational research related to a student's need for belonging in the school community, Karen Osterman found that "students who experience acceptance are more highly motivated and engaged in learning and more committed to school" (2000, p. 359). Inclusion helps all students to feel accepted and supported, meeting each child's emotional and learning needs.

Social Benefits

Prosocial skills are those behaviors that help us make friends and maintain relationships, and they are vital to our ability to connect with one another. Prosocial skills are more than just using manners and sharing. Examples of other prosocial skills include empathy, impulse control, and self-calming skills. Researchers have discovered a significant relationship between the prosocial skills that young children have and their future success. The results of a recent study published in the *American Journal of Public Health* indicate that social competence in young children has a significant impact on their future outcomes, and that they are more likely to live healthier and successful lives as adults (Jones, Greenberg, & Crowley, 2015a). This study reinforces that students of all abilities should be interacting with one another and should be given opportunities to build relationships with peers. It is important to note

Figure 1.4. Two teammates celebrate the end of a successful football game. (Contributed by Sheryl Zellis.)

that students both with and without disabilities benefit from the social interaction an inclusive classroom provides. McGregor and Vogelsberg performed a synthesis of literature to inform best practices about inclusive schooling in 1998. They found that its benefits include high levels of social interaction and the development of friendships between students with disabilities and their typical peers. Students of all abilities also benefit from social interaction when they attend general education classes together, eat lunch together, and have shared experiences such as field trips and assemblies. They know one another by name and feel confident interacting with each other, all because they have had the opportunity to be together. See Figure 1.4 for an example of this kind of positive social interaction. More recently, Wilson, Ellerbee, and Christian (2011) surveyed 16 inclusion teachers about their students with disabilities. Teachers were asked whether their students with disabilities benefited from inclusion classrooms in several areas, including behavior and social skills. Seventy-five percent of the teachers interviewed reported that their students with disabilities did benefit in the areas of behavior and social skills.

Academic Benefits

Research has proven over and over again that students with and without disabilities maintain or gain academic skills in the inclusive classroom. It has been reported that the academic achievement of typically developing students has not been compromised by the inclusion of students with disabilities in the general education classroom (Cole et al., 2004; McDonnell et al., 2003; McGregor & Vogelsberg, 1998). In a review of the effects of inclusive schooling for students, researchers found that students with disabilities educated in inclusive settings made significant progress in the areas of mathematics and reading (Cole et al., 2004). Most recently, Dessemontet, Bless, and Morin (2011) conducted a comparative study consisting of 34 children with intellectual disabilities who were fully included in general education classrooms and 34 comparable students in special schools. Their academic achievement was compared over a 2-year period. The results indicated that included children made slightly more progress in literacy skills than children attending special schools (Dessemontet et al., 2011). The researchers concluded that inclusive education is an appropriate educational option for young students with intellectual disabilities. Inclusive classrooms that provide content-rich curriculum, a variety of learning materials, and student-centered instruction have many academic benefits for students, including those students with intellectual disabilities working below grade level.

CONCLUSION

In the United States, research, experience, and federal law tell us that students with disabilities must be educated in the least restrictive environment of a general education classroom with appropriate aids and supports. Unfortunately, there are barriers to inclusive education that can derail the right of all students to a meaningful, enriching education. Although some students with disabilities have opportunities to learn in general education settings, too often we see students in situations that are not truly inclusive (i.e., integration) who miss out on the full benefits of true inclusion described previously. Remember that with authentic inclusive education, students do not have to "fit into" the preexisting conditions of the class. Rather, the classroom and school environments are designed to provide the supports and structures that every student needs to succeed. Knowing and understanding the principles of inclusion, as well as its social, emotional, and academic benefits, are essential to upholding its practice.

This chapter has provided a foundation for what genuine inclusion looks like as well as ideas about how to break down some of the barriers that prevent all students from participating in general education. Remember that inclusion is not an isolated program; rather, it is the result of a concerted, schoolwide effort to provide students with disabilities accessible and successful educational experiences. Chapter 2 will explore ways in which schools can effectively support inclusive education.

CHAPTER 2

. . . .

Supporting Inclusion Schoolwide

Inclusive education doesn't spontaneously happen. In addition to foundational beliefs and attitudes that must be held by stakeholders (see Chapter 1), inclusion requires an overall shift in how schools create and manage school culture, staffing, resources, and spaces. Every aspect of the school, from the bus driver to the learning materials to communication with families, must be prepared to support inclusion. Structures and systems are needed to support inclusive practice at the school, classroom, and curriculum levels, which together create a framework for inclusion. This framework—school, classroom, and curriculum—gives the school community guidance for how to practice inclusion; it outlines where and how students' needs are met, who meets those needs, and what types of supplemental aids and services are available.

In this chapter, you will learn about the supports that must be in place at the school level to successfully facilitate authentic inclusive education. First and foremost, schools must have solid leadership and staff who are dedicated to the principles of inclusion. These professionals work together to promote positive school culture, build a school community, and establish inclusive spaces, all of which help facilitate inclusive activities and experiences.

THE ROLE OF SCHOOL LEADERSHIP AND STAFF

To make inclusion work, educational staff need to work together to support every student's equal membership and participation in school. School leaders are particularly instrumental in establishing inclusive values and practices; their role is complemented by that of school support staff, who play a critical role in educating and supporting students with disabilities.

Administrators

The practice of inclusive education requires ongoing commitment and dedication to providing all children with an equal education. Nowhere in an inclusive school is that more necessary than in the job of the administrator. School administrators set the tone, provide direction, and oversee the daily operation of schools. Most important, school administrators can support and facilitate inclusive learning environments. Riehl (2000) observed that administrators should focus on three tasks to support the diverse needs of the student population: fostering diversity, promoting an inclusive culture and instructional programs, and building relationships between schools and communities. Overall, administrators should strive to ensure that schools are providing students with a quality, equal education in safe classrooms.

Administrators of schools ensure inclusiveness in numerous ways. For example, they help set the welcoming, friendly tone of an inclusive school by connecting with students on a daily basis. They monitor the overall academic progress of students within the school and keep informed of staff needs. Regular meetings and assemblies help entire schools and families connect, share achievements, and celebrate learning.

Administrators are also responsible for managing the resources allocated to their schools. These resources can include staffing, funding, technology, learning materials, programs, and contributions from the community. The kinds of resources available and how they are allocated can have a significant impact on the inclusion of students with disabilities, and administrators play an important role in this decision-making process. For example, having scheduled staff support or collaboration time is an essential resource needed by inclusive schools, and administrators in support of inclusion will ensure that this time is allotted.

Specialized Support Staff

School employees who give ongoing, specialized assistance with the education of students with disabilities are known as *specialized support staff*. Some examples of support staff include counselors, speech-language pathologists (SLPs), and occupational therapists. They play a vital role in the inclusion of students with disabilities. Support staff are integral members of a student's educational team. Assessment, educational program design, and communication with outside student services are some of the jobs required of school support staff.

In an inclusive school, support staff work very closely with the classroom teachers and paraprofessionals. Once a student is identified as having a learning issue and/or disability and has an education plan, the support staff collaborate with the classroom teacher and paraprofessional to ensure that the plan is delivered. Together, they assist students in various ways that are directly related to their intellectual, social, emotional, and/or physical growth. Student growth is assessed at regular intervals, and the support staff, teachers, and paraprofessionals share information about the student's growth with one another through the school year. (More information about the roles of classroom teachers and paraprofessionals in an inclusive school can be found in Chapter 3.) For example, a school counselor might support social skill development in students by creating a peer-tutoring program. Likewise, students who experience delays in speech and vocabulary development can benefit from skills of an SLP. The inclusive attitude and expertise of support staff are vital to the successful education of students in a school system.

All schools (inclusive or not) rely on some form of support staff. However, it is how those services are accessed that characterizes an inclusive school. In traditional schools, students with identified needs (e.g., a student with a reading disability) are removed from their classroom for a portion of the day to receive specialized instruction. This removal can cause a significant disruption to the student's day, particularly for a student who has more than one identified educational need. This practice of segregated education for most if not all of the day results in the student missing out on the activities of his or her regular class.

Inclusive schools work to avoid separating and segregating students from their peers for extended periods of time. Rather than having the child leave the classroom for support services, the support services are brought to the child in the classroom. Also, school support staff can support student learning through recommending the use of assistive technology. Their knowledge of technology and software is directly related to the student's area of need. The overall goal of support professionals is to assist in the child's learning and development while supporting access to and participation in the general education curriculum.

Other Important School Staff

Along with administration, teaching staff, and specialized support staff, there are staff members who help with the overall function of the school. These staff members include custodians, bus drivers, office personnel, lunch supervisors, and recess supervisors. They are not directly involved in the education of the students; however, they do interact with students as part of their job responsibilities. For example, bus drivers give students direction to keep them safe on the bus, and recess supervisors reinforce playground rules. For this reason, the attitudes and actions of the support staff have a significant impact on the inclusive environment of a school. Therefore, support staff must be trained in inclusive practice so they can help uphold the values and culture of the school. School staff must adhere to the language and behaviors that are exhibited by other members of the school community. Furthermore, school staff should also be aware of any special needs that a student with disabilities might have. For example, if a student is severely allergic to peanuts, all school employees (including both specialized and general support staff) should know the signs of anaphylaxis and how to respond appropriately. School staff are also kept abreast of relevant student information such as schedules, behavior management plans, and communication issues. It is important to an inclusive school that all the students, as well as all the staff, are participating members of the school community.

TIPS FROM AN INCLUSIVE EDUCATOR:
Understanding How Support Staff Can Help

Shortly after finishing university with my education degree in hand, I found a job teaching in a rural public school. The school had approximately 50 students enrolled at the time, with two classrooms. One classroom was for the intermediate grades and the second was for the primary grades. The primary class needed a teacher, and I was eager to fill the spot. In retrospect, I'm not sure what I was thinking when I told the principal that I could *easily* teach a primary class with four grade levels.

In my first year at the school, the principal only worked with us part time. She spent most of her time at another school site approximately 65 miles away. We saw her when the weather was decent and her schedule permitted. Our learning support teacher, SLP, and school counselor also lived 65 miles away and were subject to the same constraints as our principal. The school had the support of a secretary who worked mornings only. When at work, she could also be counted on to act as the librarian and school nurse. A paraprofessional, a custodian, a bus driver/maintenance person, and a lunchtime supervisor rounded out our school personnel.

During that year, I learned to forever appreciate any and all support from school staff! Their contribution to a student's learning experience is just as important as a classroom teacher's. In addition, their presence and behavior affects the student population. Aside from their standard job duties, support staff can help with the inclusion of students with disabilities in any of the following ways:

Providing an extra set of eyes and ears in settings where teachers are generally not present. For example, a lunch supervisor can give further insight into a student's friendships and social interactions.

Helping with the implementation of a school, class, or individual behavior program. A support teacher can help with transitions between classes or social skill development at lunchtime.

Noticing and/or affirming overall student progress. Support staff can see the translation of skills learned in the classroom into other aspects of school life. For example, a cafeteria employee who interacts daily with students who purchase lunch might notice an individual student's progress with math skills involving money.

Providing resources or expertise that a teacher may not have. I once had our school bus driver come into my classroom to give a health and safety lesson. He was a search and rescue expert in our community and taught the students how to stay safe while hiking outdoors.

Connecting with students in areas other than class curriculum. One year, I had a student who struggled to develop friendships with his classmates. However, he and our school custodian shared a passion for whales. Whenever they would pass one another in the hall, they would share a fact about the mammal. This brief conversation gave the student experience with positive and enjoyable interactions.

SCHOOL CULTURE

School culture consists of the collective norms, attitudes, ideals, and behaviors that characterize a school and are demonstrated by school leadership, teachers, students, and the larger community. In an inclusive school, school culture supports including every student in every aspect of school life. Whether it is during class time, during recess, or in the cafeteria or gymnasium, students are interacting with one another, as shown in Figure 2.1. As mentioned previously, inclusive education is not a program that happens in a select number of classrooms or for a select group of students. Instead, it is the process in which a school community welcomes every child and works toward giving students an equal opportunity to learn and participate in the curriculum and school life. There are several ways to cultivate an inclusive school culture, from attention to the school's mission statements and the language used in the school building to creating thoughtful school schedules that allow every student access to academics, events, and activities.

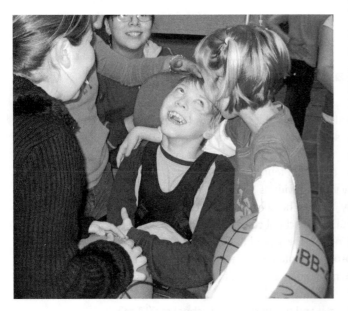

Figure 2.1. A group of friends share a laugh while practicing basketball skills. (Contributed by Renee Laporte.)

Inclusive Schools Start by Saying "Yes"

Inclusion begins by saying, "Yes, we will educate every child." Regardless of the child's abilities and issues, inclusive schools welcome all school-age children into their school community. Because there are no prerequisites for inclusion, it is assumed that every child will be educated in the general education classroom with his or her same-age peers, with appropriate supports. Once a child is a member of the school community, staff strive to support the child's needs in the best way possible. Every potential option is explored in order to uphold the child's right to a rich and meaningful education.

Inclusion also begins by saying, "Yes, every child is a valued member of our school." Every child is made to feel welcome in an inclusive school. They have the same opportunities as other students to participate in school events and activities such as assemblies. They have the same opportunities to contribute their time, talents, and skills to the overall operation of the school. For example, all students are encouraged to take on leadership roles such as library assistant or peer helper. Inclusive schools find ways for all students to participate in every aspect of school life.

Finally, inclusive schools say, "Yes, every child has unique strengths, challenges, interests, and talents. Therefore, each child will receive the educational supports and services unique to his or her needs." Not every student who needs learning support will receive the same duration and type of intervention. Some students may require more intense instruction, whereas others only need to attend a specialized reading group once a week. Inclusive schools recognize that there is no one-size-fits-all approach to educating students, and thus they tailor educational programs to best support academic, physical, emotional, and social needs.

Mission Statements

Schools reinforce an inclusive culture in many different ways, one of which includes the use of mission statements. *Mission statements* are formal summaries of an organization's values, behaviors, and purpose. In a school system, mission statements declare the school's goal in educating students and are reminders to make sure the school culture aligns with these goals. Statements are formulated through the collaboration of staff, administrators, and school community members. Gabriel and Farmer stated, "Mission statements are the 'how-to' statements or action plans that help schools achieve their vision" (2009, p. 54). Figure 2.2 shows an example of a mission statement from Twelfth Avenue Elementary School in Burnaby, British Columbia, Canada. Twelfth Avenue Elementary is an inclusive school that educates a very diverse student population. Their mission statement describes the school community and its goal in teaching all students.

**Twelfth Avenue Elementary
Mission Statement**

Twelfth Avenue Elementary Schools is a diverse, dynamic, and inclusive community.

As a team, we strive to provide a safe and structured environment, which nurtures and empowers each member of our community and challenges all of us to reach our potential.

We foster a positive self-image and equip all students with the attitudes, knowledge and skills that will enable them to become lifelong learners.

Twelfth Avenue Elementary School
Burnaby, British Columbia, Canada

Figure 2.2. Mission statement for Twelfth Avenue Elementary School. (Contributed by Marilyn Kwok.)

Language

Language is used to communicate ideas, self-express, and interact with others. In an inclusive school, the school community uses language to accept and support one another. Inclusive schools generally use *people-first language,* in which children with disabilities are seen as individuals first and foremost, regardless of disability or impairment. Words with negative connotations or that lack cultural sensitivity are not tolerated. Inclusive schools use language that avoids phrases or words that exclude groups of people. This helps avoid negative associations, connotations, and dehumanization of people with disabilities. However, it is important to mention that not everyone who is a supporter of inclusive education believes in using the same type of people-first language. As a result, the language used in an inclusive school should be agreed upon in consultation with the school community, and it should be, above all, respectful.

J. Dan Rothwell, in his 1981 book, *Telling It Like It Isn't: Language Misuse and Malpractice,* encourages us to learn to appreciate the power of language and use it responsibly. In an inclusive school, administrators, teachers, support staff, and even parents must take on the responsibility of modeling inclusive language and should expect it from their students. In fact, some schools will train their staff in using a standard inclusive language. Entire school districts often will create their own inclusive language policy. This policy sets out to identify acceptable language that can be used in all of that district's schools to support inclusion. It addresses issues such as stereotyping, demeaning words, and unnecessary references to physical characteristics. For example, Durham District School Board in Ontario, Canada, published *Guidelines for Inclusive Language Policy* (2009). This document was created to give schools direction in the type of language that is respectful and sensitive to our diverse society. In the document, some of the recommendations include avoiding the use of gender-specific phrases; for example, using *humankind* instead of *mankind,* or *workforce* instead of *manpower.*

Schedules

School schedules that are intentionally designed to suit all members of the school community also reflect an inclusive school culture. Schedules uphold the values of inclusion by providing time for staff to develop, implement, and reflect on their inclusive practice. Results from a research study on block scheduling and the impact it had on a very successful inclusive high school showed that inclusion and block scheduling at that school site were complementary and mutually supportive (Weller & McLeskey, 2000). In some cases, a school schedule will even be adapted for individual students, depending on their needs. For example, a student with disabilities may require a shortened school day. Inclusive schools also consider a student's needs for socialization, health and nutrition, and creative expression in addition to academics, and weave into the school day opportunities to educate the whole child. In this way, they create an enriching school culture in which students can develop their social, emotional, physical, and intellectual skills. In addition, school schedules can facilitate inclusion by providing the following:

- Time for collaborative planning among staff

- Time for extracurricular sports teams to meet at lunch rather than after school

- Breaks for students to eat, socialize, and move around at regular intervals. For example, some schools shorten the lunch hour to create a morning break and an afternoon break.

- Math and language arts classes offered at optimal times of the day when students are alert and motivated

- School events, such as concerts, held at various times of the day and throughout the school year to provide opportunities for all parents to attend as many events as possible

Events

A final example of ways in which a school supports inclusive culture is through the schoolwide opportunities and activities it provides for its students. In an inclusive school, events and activities appeal to a diverse group of students and are made accessible to everyone. Extracurricular clubs and sports team practices are offered at different times of the day to allow for greater student attendance (students who ride the bus home after school often miss out on after-school activities). In addition, school personnel ensure that events are accessible. At one school where I worked, the year is kicked off with a schoolwide bowling party at the local bowling alley. Although the majority of the students walked to the bowling alley, the principal arranged transportation for students who had mobility issues.

The types of clubs and sports teams are also taken into consideration at an inclusive school. Both academic and nonacademic clubs and teams are created to appeal to various student interests. A variety of activities should be offered and available to all students, such as science night, band performances, and art shows. Also, some school events should be tailored to include families. As an example, at the elementary school in my neighborhood, a family reading night is held each year. During this event, students and families are invited to listen to a well-known children's author read a story aloud. Afterward, there are books available around the room for the students to read with their friends and family.

SCHOOL COMMUNITY

The *school community* is a term that typically refers to the families, neighborhoods, businesses, and services that care about and contribute to the well-being of the school. Inclusive schools actively welcome community members in their day-to-day operations. The school community is instrumental in supporting inclusive practice and education, from volunteering in classrooms to securing resources and providing supplemental funding.

The positive effect that family involvement has on student achievement has been studied for decades. In a meta-analysis of 77 studies of more than 300,000 students, results indicated that parental involvement yields higher student achievement levels (Jeynes, 2005). Inclusive schools are aware of this positive correlation and make a point of including the community in the process of educating students by openly and regularly communicating with families. Frequent newsletters and bulletin boards provide information regarding school events and are translated into various languages. Teachers give regular updates on student progress. Parent–teacher meetings are held at crucial points in the school year (e.g., the first month of school and/or at the end of a reporting period). The school's inclusion of its surrounding community sets an overarching tone that values the meaningful participation of members. It ensures that everyone, from students to families to community members, is welcome and engaged in the learning process.

TIPS FROM AN INCLUSIVE EDUCATOR:
Connecting With the Community

We had the smallest staff and school population in the district. Most of our time and energy was spent keeping our kids learning and our classrooms running smoothly. However, as anyone who has been to school knows, there is more to school life than just sitting in a classroom. Extracurricular sports, fundraising, and special events, such as sports day, help round out the activities that are provided for students. With the help of a very active school community, we were able to give our students opportunities to learn outside the classroom.

The first year I was at the school, we planned a day of multicultural events for staff and students. The purpose was to highlight the many different cultures in our region. Feeling confident in our ability to host, we invited another small rural school in our area to participate. The plan was to set up seven or eight stations around the gymnasium. Each station would have a different cultural activity for the students to experience. Some of the stations included food, art, and music. As the planning got under way, we quickly realized that our small staff was not very culturally diverse! We would not be able to give an accurate representation of our area. More help was needed.

Invitations to participate were sent out to community members. Soon enough, the lady who worked at the post office, a bus driver, and a local farmer were among the eager respondents. Things were looking up! After reviewing our list of activities, however, we discovered that we still didn't have a food station. So, I did what most teachers would do and I volunteered my spouse. His Hungarian background and love of cooking made him a perfect choice. (To this day, we still talk about the night he stayed up making over 200 breaded chicken cutlets for the students to eat.) The multicultural day went off without a hitch and we couldn't have done it without the help of our school community (and, of course, my husband).

Based on this experience, I recommend keeping the following points in mind:

- Your school community comprises many unique individuals. Although not directly involved in day-to-day school activities, they may nevertheless be able to make important contributions or meet highly specific needs.

- Make use of all available communication resources (e.g., mail, e-mail, your school website, social media) to reach out to community members you may not know (yet) and give them opportunities to get involved.

- Sometimes, we overlook resources that may be right next door to us—or closer. A neighbor, a friend, or even a spouse may unexpectedly prove to be just the right person to fill a specific need.

SCHOOL SPACES

In addition to federal laws ensuring that people with disabilities have access to public places, inclusive schools create a sense of belonging and inclusion through building design, furniture, and materials. Inclusive school spaces are a physical, tangible reflection of the belief system that the school community holds. Classrooms, libraries, auditoriums, and playgrounds are responsive to the students' interests and needs by using a multitude of ways to physically facilitate feelings of inclusion and belonging. See Table 2.1 for a list of ideas for making inclusive school spaces. Inclusive spaces also promote opportunities for cognitive, social, emotional, and physical growth and are designed with the diverse cultures and languages of students in mind.

Table 2.1. Inclusive school spaces

Area of school	Ideas for inclusion
Front office	• Post a welcome sign in different languages. • Provide newsletters and community notices (translated if necessary) and post online. • Post a school event board to notify staff and community of upcoming events. • Display student artwork and projects. • Post photos of school events. • Notify the community of school awards and achievements. • Have a morning greeting from the principal, a staff member, or a student. • Have the daily bulletin read by students and post it online. • Make birthday announcements.
Library	• Provide various print, audio, and visual materials. • Ensure that technology is up to date and available. • Offer a reading club that is open to all students. • Have student assistants help with younger grades. • Create a "reading buddies" program. • Provide workspaces for group and/or individual projects. • Ensure that shelving and books are accessible. • Offer different types of seating and seating arrangements. • Create silent reading areas. • Provide different types of lighting.
Playground	• Ensure that pathways to and around the playground are accessible. • Provide modified playground equipment. • Make sports equipment available to students. • Create an area for structured games. • Provide a group seating area. • Make use of a playground social coordinator who organizes games and activities for students. • Create quiet areas for students to read or chat.
Classroom	• Group desks together to facilitate group interaction. • Provide large tables for cooperative group work. • Ensure that shelving is appropriate for student reach. • Designate an area for class meetings and discussions. • Create learning centers such as a book nook, science station, or writing retreat. • Use masking tape to outline walkways and student seating. • Supply materials for differentiated learning. • Provide different types of lighting in the room. • Post visual reminders, announcements, and lesson concepts. • Communicate regularly with families.

CONCLUSION

A school's job is not solely the education of its students. Rather, schools should connect people, support students, celebrate learning, and embrace communities. Above all, schools set the tone for inclusive education. School staff, particularly administrators, play a leading role in establishing a welcoming, accepting school culture and community where all students feel valued. Inclusive schools depend on respectful language and a shared commitment to each child's social, emotional, academic, and physical development. Schools with inclusive values also look to the larger community for assistance with funding, resources, volunteer time, and advocacy, modeling inclusion by inviting all community members to participate and contribute to daily operations. Finally, inclusive schools provide flexible scheduling for classes, events, and activities, as well as accessible spaces that meet the needs of all learners, from the classroom to the gym to the cafeteria.

Now that we have discussed inclusive education at the school level, it's time to take a look at how inclusive education works in the individual classroom. Chapter 3 discusses the supports and classroom structures that every teacher needs in order to include students of all abilities in the general education curriculum.

CHAPTER 3

· · · · · · · · · · ·

Supporting Inclusion in the Classroom

As discussed in Chapter 2, certain supports are required in a school to successfully include students. Inclusion is largely dependent on the support of administration and school personnel. The language, schedules, events, and school spaces also facilitate a welcoming culture where all students feel valued and respected. Finally, the school needs support from the community, which gives valuable assistance with funding, resources, volunteer time, and advocacy.

In addition to establishing inclusive practices at the school level, it is important to provide supports for inclusive education within each classroom. In this chapter, we will examine classroom structures that facilitate inclusion, beginning with the people responsible for making inclusion happen daily. The chapter opens with an overview of the roles and responsibilities that the classroom teacher, co-teacher, and paraprofessional have in making an inclusive classroom run smoothly. I will also discuss the role that families and community volunteers have at the classroom level—not to mention the vital role that built-in peer supports play in the inclusive classroom culture. Finally, I will discuss how to establish and maintain an inclusive classroom culture. This is accomplished through establishing a strength-based classroom; cultivating a climate of acceptance; supporting students' social-emotional development; taking a positive, proactive approach to classroom management; and responding appropriately to student needs.

THE INCLUSIVE CLASSROOM TEAM: BUILDING A NETWORK OF SUPPORT

Successful inclusion in the classroom depends on the collaboration and expertise of a range of professionals (e.g., co-teacher/special educator, paraprofessionals), not just the classroom teacher. Equally important are contributions from family and community members, who provide advice on meeting the needs of individual students (e.g., through membership on the individualized education program [IEP] team) and assist in daily classroom operations. Finally, peers are a natural form of support for students with disabilities—through reciprocal relationships, children both with and without disabilities benefit from one another socially and academically. The sections that follow discuss the roles and necessary skills of each of these key team players who together help to uphold inclusive practices at the classroom level.

The Classroom Teacher

The knowledge and confidence that a general education teacher has with inclusive practice have a significant impact on the success of an inclusive learning environment (Forlin, Loreman, Sharma, & Earle, 2009). For successful inclusive education, teachers need to have some form of training in inclusive schooling. In his model for teacher preparation on inclusion, Whitworth (1999) tells us that there are three components to an effective preservice program:

1. Preservice teachers need **opportunities for collaborative teaching,** such as co-teaching, collaborative planning, and collaborative assessment.

2. Preservice teachers need to learn the **techniques and strategies for teaching in an inclusive classroom.** Teachers need to feel comfortable with providing accommodations, inclusive instruction, and modified materials.

3. Preservice teachers need **practice and multiple experiences** with teaching in an inclusive classroom.

Keep in mind that it takes more than a course in inclusive education to adequately prepare teachers for inclusion. Training teachers for inclusion involves sharing knowledge, shaping belief systems, mentoring, and providing actual classroom experiences. Note that the learning does not end once the training is over. Teaching is a lifelong process of learning how to best meet the needs of students, classrooms, and schools. Inclusive schools often host workshops and discussions that help teachers address questions and issues in the classroom.

Inclusive teachers see one another as members of the same team. They share ideas, instructional strategies, and even classrooms. As an example, for several years I collaborated with a colleague who taught the same grade as I did. At the beginning of each school year, we assessed our students' overall performance in the subject of math. We would then place students into one of three groups based on their ability level. My colleague would teach the group of students who were performing above grade level, I taught the group that was working right at grade level, and we arranged for the school's special education teacher to work with the students who were working significantly below grade level.

Another defining characteristic of inclusive teachers is that they take primary responsibility for educating all students, including those with disabilities. With the support of specialized school staff, inclusive classroom teachers deliver and assess instruction to students in the most effective way possible. Some of these methods include *universal design for learning* (UDL) with *differentiated instruction* (which will be discussed further in Chapter 4). They facilitate instruction and learning through the use of inclusive spaces, materials, and resources.

Finally, and most notably, classroom teachers model inclusive behavior and set similar expectations for members of the class. Through class routines, discussions, and activities, inclusive teachers engage students in respectful and meaningful interaction with one another. For example, students with and without disabilities are not only in the same class but they also eat lunch and have recess together. Furthermore, these are not contrived or forced experiences in which one student helps out another by being a buddy or lunch partner.

The Co-Teacher

Co-teachers are teaching professionals who help support and facilitate student access to the curriculum. In most schools, co-teachers are also the special education or learning support teachers. They devote their day to helping students and teachers throughout the school. Note that co-teaching is not synonymous with collaborative or shared classroom teaching models, in which teachers share equally the responsibility for teaching the general education curriculum to typically developing students as well as students with disabilities. In contrast, a co-teacher generally has less direct responsibility for shaping the general education curriculum but plays a vital role in implementing this curriculum with students whose educational needs differ from those of typically developing students. Co-teachers have specialized training and knowledge that can enhance a student's learning experience in the general education classroom. According to Zigmond and Magiera:

> Co-teaching draws on the strengths of both the general educator, who understands the structure, content, and pacing of the general education curriculum, and the special educator, who can identify unique learning needs of individual students and enhance curriculum and instruction to match these needs. (2001, p. 2)

The type of support that a co-teacher provides for students is typically intensive, specialized, and tailored to a student's learning goals. It can be in a one-to-one format or small-group setting for a period of time during the school day. Friend, Cook, Hurley-Chamberlain, and Shamberger propose six different models for co-teaching. In short, they are:

1. **One teach/one observe**–One teacher teaches the class while the other teacher observes students and collects data.

2. **One teach/one assist**–One teacher teaches the class while the other teacher walks around the class assisting students.

3. **Parallel teaching**–One teacher teaches half the class while the other teaches the remaining students.

4. **Station teaching**–One teacher instructs small groups of students for one portion of the lesson and then sends them on to the other teacher to learn the remaining material.

5. **Alternate teaching**–One teacher leaves the room with a group of students to provide them with more explicit, direct instruction.

6. **Team teaching**–Both teachers share responsibility for delivering and planning instruction. (2010, p. 12)

Regardless of the co-teaching model used, however, the instruction provided by both teachers is purposeful and research based. Typically, the co-teacher will also assist in assessing and reporting the progress of students in the area in which they received extra support. Co-teachers can help track compliance with student IEPs or Section 504 plans. Finally, the collaborative nature of a co-teaching model can provide both teachers with an opportunity for professional development.

Several authors have written extensively on the topic of co-teaching and have produced books for education professionals. For teachers who are new to co-teaching or are looking to improve their current practice, it is well worth the time to look for these resources. They will provide a more thorough understanding of the processes involved in co-teaching, as well as the advantages, pitfalls, and tips for success. Some of those resources are noted in Appendix A.

The Paraprofessional

A paraprofessional is a trained adult whose job is to help the student(s) with disabilities. Paraprofessionals help the students access curricula and school life. In addition, some paraprofessionals provide assistance during school time with the student's functional life skills. The type, duration, and extent of the support are determined by the student's physical, intellectual, and/or social-emotional goals. These goals and supports are identified and prioritized by the school-based team and recorded on the student's IEP. The paraprofessional, with the guidance of the classroom teacher and special education teacher, then uses his or her skill set to implement the supports and meet the student's IEP goals.

A paraprofessional does not replace the classroom teacher and is not responsible for determining educational programming and goals. Rather, a paraprofessional facilitates the individual educational goals recorded in the student's IEP. Paraprofessionals are also not expected to create a separate classroom curriculum for the student in an inclusive class. Instead, in collaboration with the teacher and special education teacher, a paraprofessional will help the student access the curriculum through accommodations and modifications to subject matter as necessary.

In addition to supporting students in learning the academic curriculum, paraprofessionals will often facilitate access to the "hidden curriculum" of the classroom. The hidden curriculum is considered to be the social and cultural rules of a school and/or classroom that are not taught but are implied. Because paraprofessionals work in close collaboration with students, they can provide advice, model behavior, and assist with communication skills. The paraprofessional can use visual prompts, facial cues, and social stories to help a student interact with his or her peers.

When a paraprofessional supports a student with special needs, there can be concern as to whether the paraprofessional is helping or hindering. There is a fine line that exists concerning how much assistance and guidance the student needs, and too much or too little can limit a student's growth. Paraprofessionals, ideally, should offer support but not take over, redo, rework, or refine. They do not act as gatekeepers or barriers to classroom and curriculum. Together, the paraprofessional and the teacher work to deliver the best possible inclusive education program to a student with disabilities. Table 3.1 suggests some ways in which teachers and paraprofessionals can establish a positive working relationship. (For more on working with paraprofessionals, see Julie Causton and Chelsea P. Tracy-Bronson's 2015 book *The Educator's Handbook for Inclusive School Practices*.)

Families

Who knows a student better than that child's parents? Inclusive schools respect the insight parents or guardians provide about their child's abilities and needs. Teachers welcome them as members of the child's educational team. The wealth of information that parents can share significantly helps a teacher plan appropriate educational support and activities. In addition, parents can be valuable resources by assisting with daily classroom activities and special events.

Even before the school year gets into full swing, you will find teachers sending home forms and arranging private meetings with families. These meetings are sometimes known as *intake meetings* and usually happen within the first 2 months of school. Questionnaires are sent home asking about student interests, strengths, and areas for further development. Figure 3.1 is an example of an interest inventory that teachers can use to gather information from parents. This form (Getting to Know Your Child; Appendix B, Form 1) can be handed out at the beginning of the year. Some teachers create another version halfway through the

Table 3.1. Tips for teachers to establish a positive working relationship with paraprofessionals

Be welcoming	Introduce yourself and welcome the paraprofessional to your class. It is his or her work environment as well, and the paraprofessional should feel comfortable and included.
Establish a workspace	Ask about the paraprofessional's preferred workspace. Some paraprofessionals like to have their own desk, work from a student desk, or carry around a bag or basket.
Discuss strengths and skill sets	Identify areas of strength and interests that the paraprofessional can bring to the classroom. Discuss any personal preferences the paraprofessional might have and ask what has worked for him or her in the past.
Tour the classroom	Show the paraprofessional around your classroom. Point out where important materials and resources are kept.
Communicate classroom expectations	Share one another's classroom philosophy and teaching style, expectations of students, behavior management, and general routines. Talk about the levels of support that the paraprofessional can provide. For example, will the paraprofessional sit next to the student or sit a few feet away and help when necessary?
Share resources	Share any relevant resources that might be helpful to the paraprofessional. Provide him or her with a copy of the curriculum plans for the year, the weekly and daily schedule, and most important, a copy of the student's individual education program. Be sure to share any ideas and tips learned from workshops and meetings throughout the year.
Give credit where credit is due	Recognize the experience and expertise of the paraprofessional. Listen to suggestions and take advice where necessary. Don't assume the paraprofessional's level of education and expertise is any less than yours. Many paraprofessionals have come from other careers, have varied backgrounds, or have their own children with disabilities.
Identify areas for support	Be aware of any challenges that the paraprofessional is facing. Be supportive and help when necessary.
Establish ongoing communication	Set up lines of communication with the paraprofessional. Make time to meet to check in and discuss areas of concern or needs.
Plan together	Most important, plan the student's program together. Collaborate on ways to meet the needs of the child, discuss the support systems that need to be in place, and review the child's progress on a regular basis.

year for parents to provide any updates. Both teachers and parents appreciate this process. The tone of interest and respect opens the door to communication about the child's development throughout the school year. Also, it is a proactive step toward identifying any issues that may arise. For example, parents can express their concern over their child's social skills and ability to make friends. The teacher can respond by embedding a social skills program in the curriculum. Reviewing the family's information about the student gives teachers a well-rounded understanding of each child in their classroom, and meeting with parents or other caregivers provides further insight and allows for discussion of questions and concerns.

Overall, family and parent involvement in a student's education is crucial. A meta-analysis of 41 studies done by Jeynes found, "a considerable and consistent relationship between parental involvement and academic achievement among urban students" (2005, p. 258) and, "programs meant to encourage parental support in their child's schooling appear positively related to achievement for urban children" (2005, p. 260). It is important to note that Jeynes' results also indicated that the positive effects of parental involvement seem to transcend differences in socioeconomics and race.

Getting to Know Your Child

This information will help me teach your child this year!

Child's name (preferred name) is _____

List three to five words that describe your child's character. _____

_____

What are your child's strengths? _____

_____

What are your child's favorite activities? _____

_____

Who are your child's friends?_____

What are your child's favorite subjects in school? _____

_____

What are your child's least favorite subjects in school? _____

_____

Do you have any concerns about your child's progress in school?_____

_____

What hopes or goals do you have for your child this year? _____

_____

Do you have any other information you would like to share?

_____

_____

Thank you!

Figure 3.1. An example of a questionnaire that can be given to parents at the beginning of the school year. The questionnaire helps teachers to collect information about students in their classes. See Form 1, Getting to Know Your Child, in Appendix B.

Volunteers

Volunteers are a much-needed support system in inclusive schools. Whether they are parents of attending students or community members, their role is invaluable. Schools often will use volunteers to help in classrooms, the library, the lunchroom, and on field trips and to help with fundraising events. There are many evening or after-school activities that schools host in which they might recruit the help of volunteers. Some volunteers help by creating class materials at home and then sending them back to the school. As with students, volunteers should be made to feel welcome in the inclusive school system.

By opening its doors to volunteers, a school makes families and the community privy to school life. Volunteers have a chance to see some of the daily challenges, celebrations, and needs within classrooms. For those reasons, volunteers often become allies and advocates for the education system. Similarly, in an economy where resources for schools can be scarce, I have seen parent committees revitalize playgrounds, populate libraries, and rebuild computer labs. Never underestimate the value of help from a volunteer!

Peers

The inclusion of students with disabilities in the general education classroom not only provides all students access to a broad, rich curriculum, but also serves as an opportunity for students with disabilities to interact with typically developing peers. In the inclusive classroom, students can be seen sitting in groups with one another, working collaboratively on a project, or discussing an assignment. All of these genuine activities with same-age peers result in social and emotional gains. Data collected from a study of students with learning disabilities showed that students who were educated in general education classrooms were more accepted by their peers, had better relationships, were less lonely, and had fewer behavior problems than students with similar challenges who were educated in a separate setting (Wiener & Tardif, 2004). Because direct instruction from teachers is not the only method of delivering curriculum in an inclusive class, peers can provide a valuable and natural system for transferring knowledge. Teachers can bring groups of students of various abilities together to learn from one another or learn together. Research shows that peer tutoring is most successful when students of different ability levels work with one another (Kunsch, Jitendra, & Sood, 2007). Even more noteworthy are the findings in a 2010 synthesis of literature on the academic effects that peer tutoring has on students with disabilities. The literature overwhelmingly reveals that peer tutoring has a positive effect on the academic outcome of students with disabilities in Grades 6 through 12 (Okilwa & Shelby, 2010).

Let's not forget that a student with disabilities can also provide peer support for his or her classmates. Students with disabilities should have an equal opportunity to share their skills and talents for the benefit of peers. Through this reciprocal relationship, friendships can form that otherwise might not have a chance to develop. Autism advocate Judy Endow tells us, "I knew that I was the only kid in the class who could never be counted as a peer to anyone else. I also could never be the recess buddy or lunch partner – only the kid who needed one" (2013, para. 5). If we want students to include, encourage, and help one another, they have to view one another as equal, not less. An example of this kind of relationship is shown in Figure 3.2, in which Nathan and his friends pose for a high school graduation picture.

Figure 3.2. Nathan and his friends pose for a high school graduation photo. (Contributed by Renee Laporte.)

CREATING AN INCLUSIVE CLASSROOM CULTURE

One of my favorite quotes about education is, "My teacher said I was smart, so I was." The only credited source is "a 6-year-old." If true, then a very insightful 6-year-old has perfectly summed up the culture of an inclusive classroom. Much like school culture, *classroom culture* is the collective beliefs, attitudes, and behaviors of the teacher and students. Inclusive classrooms welcome all students, create opportunities for all students to participate in learning, and are respectful of diversity. Inclusive classrooms support the abilities—and recognize the possibilities—of all students, not only academically but also in terms of social-emotional growth. You can create an inclusive classroom culture by establishing a strength-based classroom, supporting students' social-emotional development, and adopting a positive classroom management style.

Establish a Strength-Based Classroom

In a *strength-based classroom,* there is a shift in thinking about student abilities. The teacher assesses what the student is capable of doing and has the potential to do in the future. Rather than letting the child's deficits or medical label define his or her potential as a learner, a strength-based classroom presumes competence. According to Lopez and Louis,

> Strength-based education begins with educators discovering what they do best and developing and applying their strengths as they help students identify and apply their strengths in the learning process so that they can reach previously unattained levels of personal excellence (2009, p. 2).

• •

In a strength-based classroom, teachers view student learning and development as dynamic. Teachers believe that students grow and learn at different rates, in different ways, and under different circumstances. What works for one child may not work for another. Dr. Gordon F. Sherman, a leader in the field of dyslexia research and education, called these variations in learning "cerebrodiversity" (Cowen, 2016), a positive and strength-based approach that differs greatly from how learning differences are traditionally viewed. Typically, schools have perceived vast differences in learning as a disability. However, when teachers view students with a strength-based mindset, they seek to celebrate, support, and accommodate learning differences. Through educational assessment and data collection, teachers and education specialists can apply strategies that are more appropriate and meaningful to that individual student's development. With differences addressed and accommodated for, students can continue to participate and advance through the education program. They can realize their potential as learners and prepare for life beyond school. Isn't that the goal of any classroom?

Support Social-Emotional Development

Inclusive classrooms are not only places to learn math, reading, and writing, but also places where students have the opportunity to grow as human beings. Educators know this type of personal growth as *social-emotional development.* The diverse nature of an inclusive environment provides a natural opportunity for social and emotional learning. An example of this is shown in Figure 3.3, in which Patrick and friends take a break from their classwork and have some fun with duct tape.

It is widely accepted that social-emotional development stems from learning how to control one's emotions, empathize with others, set and achieve goals, and have positive relationships, as well as learning how to maintain those positive relationships (Elias et al., 1997). Students with strong prosocial skills exhibit a greater acceptance of their peers (Newcomb, Bukowski, & Pattee, 1993) and decreased incidents of bullying (Frey et al., 2005). Most important, a recent research study showed that young children with well-developed social competence skills are more likely to live healthier, successful lives as adults (Jones, Greenberg, & Crowley, 2015b).

In addition to the natural opportunities for social-emotional learning that inclusive classrooms offer, it has been recommended that students also receive formal instruction in this area. Studies have shown that it is imperative to have direct social-emotional programming integrated into the school experience so students can prepare for adult life in a global world (Katz & Porath, 2011). Inclusive educators can teach and reinforce social-emotional development by providing instruction on social skills that meets the needs of a broad range of students in the classroom. Sometimes, these

Figure 3.3. Patrick and friends take a break from their classwork and have some fun with duct tape. (Photo taken by Sarah Barnes. Contributed by Beth Foraker.)

programs focus lessons on a subset of skills, such as turn taking. Other programs tackle larger concepts of character development, such as integrity, honesty, and perseverance. There are currently more than 200 recognized social-emotional learning programs used in schools across North America (Durlak, Weissberg, Dymnicki, Taylor, & Schellinger, 2011). Some of the more effective programs are The Leader in Me (Covey, 2014), Roots of Empathy (Gordon, 2012), and Tribes Learning Communities (Gibbs, 2006). The Collaborative for Academic, Social, and Emotional Learning (CASEL, 2017) provides a more comprehensive overview of social and emotional learning programs in their 2017 guides, which can be found online at www.casel.org/guide/.

Outside of structured programs, educators can also teach social skill development through experiential activities. Consider using the following eight ideas to cultivate social and emotional skills in your inclusive classroom.

1. **Model manners.** Teachers support inclusion in their classrooms by modeling inclusive behavior and language. If teachers expect their students to learn and display good social skills, then they need to lead by example. A teacher's welcoming attitude sets the tone of behavior among the students. They learn how to socialize and respect one another from the teacher's example. For instance, teachers should not be yelling to get students' attention and then expect students to be respectful of one another.

2. **Assign classroom jobs.** Classroom jobs provide students with opportunities to demonstrate responsibility, teamwork, and leadership. Jobs such as handing out papers, taking attendance, and being a line-leader can highlight a student's strengths and build confidence. This practice also helps alleviate the workload! Teachers often will rotate class jobs to ensure that every student has an opportunity to participate.

3. **Role-play.** As any teacher knows, it's important to teach students a concept and then give them an opportunity to practice the skill and demonstrate their understanding. The same holds true for teaching social skills. A common teaching strategy that teachers use is to have students practice social skills through role playing. Teachers can provide structured scenarios in which the students can act out various social situations, and then the teacher can offer immediate feedback.

4. **Arrange a pen pal program.** For years, I arranged a pen pal program in my class. Students from my class wrote letters to students in another class at another school. This activity was a favorite of mine. It taught students how to demonstrate proactive social skills through written communication. Especially valuable for introverted personalities, writing letters gives students time to collect their thoughts. It levels the playing field for students who do not speak. I was also able to provide structured sentence frames in which the students held polite conversation with their pen pals. Setting up a pen pal program in your classroom takes some preparation before the letter writing begins. In particular, teachers need to give guidelines on language usage, topics, and how much personal information to share.

5. **Provide large- and small-group experiences.** In addition to their academic benefits, large- and small-group activities can give students an opportunity to develop teamwork skills, goal setting, and responsibility. Students are often assigned roles to uphold within the group such as reporter, scribe, or timekeeper. At times, these groups are self-determined and sometimes they are prearranged. Group work can also help quieter students connect with others; it appeals to extroverts and reinforces respectful behavior. Examples of large-group activities are group discussions, group projects,

and games. Small-group activities can be used for more detailed assignments or activities. Before any group work takes place in the class, it is a good idea for the teacher to review group behavior and expectations.

6. **Establish a big buddy system.** In terms of social skills, it is just as important for students to know how to communicate with younger or older people as it is with their peers. The big buddy system is a great way for students to learn how to interact with different age groups. In a big buddy situation, an older class will pair up with a younger class for an art project, reading time, or games. Again, this type of activity needs to be preplanned and carefully designed with students' strengths and interests in mind. Classroom teachers meet ahead of time to create pairings of students and to prepare a structured activity. There is also time set aside for the teacher to set guidelines for interaction and ideas for conversation topics. Entire schools have implemented buddy programs to enrich their students' lives.

7. **Read, write, or tell stories that teach social skills.** There are dozens of stories for kids that teach social skills in direct or indirect ways. Stories written expressly for this purpose are known as social stories (Gray, 2010) or social narratives. Find ways to incorporate these stories in your class programs. You can set aside some time each day to read aloud a story to the class or use a story during instructional time. Better yet, have your class write stories with characters that display certain character traits.

8. **Hold class meetings.** Class meetings are a wonderful way to teach students how to be diplomatic, show leadership, solve problems, and take responsibility. They are usually held weekly and are a time for students to discuss current classroom events and issues. Successful and productive meetings involve discussions centered on classroom concerns and not individual problems. Also, these meetings reinforce the value that each person brings to the class. Before a class meeting, teachers can provide the students with group guidelines for behavior, prompts, and sentence frames to facilitate meaningful conversation.

Adopt a Positive Classroom Management Style

Classroom management is more than just rewarding good behavior and giving detentions. It is a systematic way of providing predictable routines, lessons, and activities that keep students engaged in learning within a safe environment. The *Glossary of Education Reform* defines *classroom management* as "the wide variety of skills and techniques that teachers use to keep students organized, orderly, focused, attentive, on task, and academically productive during a class" ("Classroom Management," 2014). Teachers, particularly those working in inclusive classrooms, must adopt a classroom management style that is responsive to the needs of such a diverse group of students. Inclusive classrooms are diverse not only in student ability but also in language, culture, and student experience. They are hubs of activity with students learning at different rates, at different times, and in different ways. There is student movement throughout the classroom as students move between activities. There are various supplies and learning materials that need to be deployed, depending on the lesson. In addition, students are given the opportunity to interact with one another through group work and cooperative learning activities.

Given the intensity of student needs and pace of activity in an inclusive classroom, there must be routines and expectations aligned with the principles of inclusion. According to prominent inclusive education expert Leslie Soodak (2003), a classroom management style that promotes community building, friendships, collaboration, parent participation, and a positive behavior management system is consistent with the goals of inclusive education. Therefore, inclusive teachers need to avoid punitive and exclusionary classroom management techniques such as isolating, humiliating, or disrespecting a student.

TIPS FROM AN INCLUSIVE EDUCATOR:

Building Your Classroom's Infrastructure

I vividly remember my first day teaching my primary class. It was a disaster. I would like to say that I was able to put to use all my handy inclusive teaching skills, but that didn't happen. In fact, I didn't get a chance to teach at all that day. I just spent it watching all my fabulous plans fall apart. As I tried to teach six different subjects to four different grades, I was painfully aware that the only thing the kids were learning was how to use the bathroom pass to escape the chaos in the classroom. We reached the end of the school day and I collapsed, thinking long and hard about my fledgling teaching career.

The following morning, I had a new plan in hand and felt confident that the students would be more engaged and attentive. We got straight to work, but things began to fall apart again. With the various attention spans, interests, abilities, and needs in the class, I couldn't keep anyone engaged in the task at hand. The younger students wanted me to tie their shoes, help spell their name, read instructions, open the paint jars, and sharpen their pencils. Meanwhile, the older students became bored quickly, chatted with one another, and wandered the classroom. Struggling to bring some sense of purpose and order back into the room, I realized why my well-thought-out lessons were falling apart. I hadn't taken the time to get to know the students, their interests, or their abilities. I hadn't established any class routines such as when to sharpen pencils (ideally, not while I'm trying to give a lesson) or what to do if and when students completed their work. I hadn't taken the time to develop any classroom infrastructure, expectations, or routines.

Setting up your classroom for a diverse group of students with a variety of ability levels and needs can be challenging, particularly if you are a first-time teacher or are new to inclusion. In addition to the assistance of the school, it is important for the classroom to provide supports for inclusion. In my first job, I underestimated the importance of providing a foundation on which to teach such a span of abilities. While trying to provide appropriate instruction for the individual grades, I glossed over the basics. I didn't pay attention to getting to know the students and establishing class guidelines, such as behavior, routines, and acceptable language. Adopting a positive, proactive classroom management style also creates a greater level of inclusion, because students know the class expectations, feel secure, and feel valued. Here are some tips for developing a solid infrastructure in your classroom where all students feel safe, welcome, and supported to learn:

Establish clear expectations for student behavior. Ensure that students understand the meaning and purpose of each expectation. For example, students need to know what you expect when you ask them to pay attention. Does that mean they stop talking? Do they look at you? Do they put their pencils down? It's important to be very clear about what each expectation looks like and sounds like.

Develop and implement routines for students to safely move and learn in the classroom. Some routines might include lining up for exiting the room for recess, handing in homework, or returning library books. Again, as with the behavior expectations, provide students with the opportunity to learn the routines and practice them. For example, on the first day of school, I would show the students how to enter the classroom safely by lining up and walking in single file. The students were given time to practice this routine so they fully understood how it worked.

Keep tasks clear and manageable. Break down instruction, requests, and explanations into chunks and tell students the expected outcomes. Make use of visuals, lists, charts, and diagrams to convey the information.

Use language that is meaningful, respectful, and positive when interacting with students. Be specific about their accomplishments (i.e., "I'm impressed that you were able to solve that math problem!" instead of "Awesome!"). Positive reinforcement and behavior modification encourage student success, whereas frequent reprimands, low expectations, and infrequent praise can result in inappropriate behavior (Aron & Loprest, 2012; Morgan, 2006).

Share the schedule of daily activities with students and families. Inform students about daily lessons and activities ahead of time by posting a daily schedule. Let both students and parents know about important events such as assemblies, tests, and celebrations. Distribute information in a way that is convenient and accessible, such as a class web site or chat. Communication apps can keep families and school connected; as of this writing, *ClassDojo* and *Bloomz* are two useful apps available for this purpose.

Reflect and Respond to Student Needs

Teacher reflection is the deliberate thinking about the choices we make as educators and how they affect our students' education. It begins by a teacher noticing a dilemma that a student faces and then proceeding to gather information about the situation. After gathering the facts, the teacher looks for solutions and weighs the options and consequences of implementing those choices. Once implemented, the teacher again reflects on the success of the solution.

Educators who work in inclusive classrooms are constantly thinking about the needs of their students. Inclusive educators wonder if they are delivering instruction that reaches all their students, and they are always thinking about ways to improve student access to curriculum. When a student requires extra support for success, teachers and school-based support teams can look to techniques such as the following:

- A change in the physical environment

- One-to-one instruction

- *Positive behavior support,* or PBS (also commonly referred to as *positive behavioral interventions and supports,* or PBIS), in which a specific student behavior, such as shouting out in class, is analyzed to determine its function, which allows educators to determine how best to support the student in learning more adaptive behavior

- Executive function skill acquisition, which addresses skills such as planning, paying attention, organization, focusing on a task, managing time and resources, and setting and attaining goals—in short, the skills that allow people to get things done

- Development of peer relationships

Consider this example of how a teacher responds to a student need. A student is observed having difficulty finishing work during the allotted time. The teacher realizes that the student sits near a window. She sees that outside noises and movement frequently distract the student. To reduce the level of distraction and improve the student's rate of task completion, the teacher moves the student's desk to the other side of the classroom and away from the window. Ultimately, an inclusive teacher reflects on and responds to a student's needs in order to keep him or her learning, interacting, and socializing in the general education classroom with the goal of avoiding exclusion or expulsion.

CONCLUSION

In an inclusive classroom, teachers, co-teachers, paraprofessionals, families, and volunteers work together to best meet the needs of all students. Collectively, all members of the inclusive team, including peers, create a culture of belonging by modeling acceptance and respect for each person involved in the classroom. Students best benefit from classrooms that consider their social, emotional, and physical needs as well as their academic growth, so teachers use positive classroom management techniques to create a safe and supportive learning environment. Finally, inclusive classrooms subscribe to a strength-based mindset, tailoring instruction and the curriculum to accommodate diverse learning styles and cater to the abilities of all learners. In Chapter 4, you will learn more about the instructional supports that allow all students access to the general education curriculum.

CHAPTER 4

. . . .

Making Curriculum Accessible Through Instructional Strategies and Accommodations

Chapters 2 and 3 illustrated the school and classroom structures needed to support a fully inclusive environment. Both must welcome students of all abilities and provide support for learning and behavior needs, as well as incorporate spaces that will facilitate inclusion. Inclusion, at the school level, is also reliant on school leadership, staff training, and collaboration. Classrooms subscribe to a strength-based mindset. Teachers, support staff, parents, and peers create a culture of belonging. Every student has an opportunity to learn.

Inclusion means more than just attending your neighborhood school, participating in assemblies, or being in the same class as your friend. It also extends into the curriculum, which comprises the lessons, activities, and experiences students have in the classroom. Participating in and learning from a robust, meaningful curriculum is one of the most significant reasons for inclusion.

Within these lively and dynamic inclusive classrooms, the way students access curriculum is contingent not only on their abilities but also on the way the material is presented. Inclusive instructional frameworks of strategies and accommodations can be used to help students access curriculum, whether or not they are working below grade level. Teachers can no longer use a one-size-fits-all approach to teaching. Our classrooms are not homogenous in terms of ability, religion, culture, or language. All students benefit from instructional strategies that are responsive and inclusive. For example, a student who is learning to speak English could use the additional support of pictures and illustrations to convey the meaning of a lesson.

Why is inclusion in curriculum so important? Providing all students with access to dynamic, productive learning environments helps to ensure that they develop knowledge and skills sets that will assist them in graduating from high school and finding future employment. According to data collected by the U.S. Department of Education, 62% of students with disabilities graduated during the 2012–2013 school year, a 3% increase over the previous 3 years (American Speech-Language-Hearing Association, 2015). In comparison, the proportion of all students who graduated that same year was 81%. Although there is still a gap between both populations, the trend of students with disabilities graduating from high school is on the rise. Furthermore, there has been a slight increase in employment rates among people with disabilities over the past 2 years, moving from a monthly employment-to-population ratio of 27.0% in 2015 to 27.7% in 2016 (Kessler Foundation, 2017). In the same report, John O'Neill, Ph.D., Director of Employment and Disability Research at Kessler Foundation, stated, "Looking at 2015 and 2016, it's clear that the job climate has improved for people with and without disabilities."

Placement in inclusive classrooms also does not disrupt or interfere with the academic outcomes of students without disabilities. In their study on the effects of inclusion on the academic performance of classmates without disabilities, Sharpe, York, and Knight (1994) discovered that there was no change in performance levels of classes with or without students with disabilities. In 2007, researchers from the University of Manchester drew a similar conclusion through a systematic review of studies that focused on the academic development of students without disabilities in inclusive classrooms. In 26 studies, they found that nondisabled students either experienced no effects (58% of studies) or positive effects (23% of studies) (Kalambouka, Farrell, Dyson, & Kaplan, 2007). With the academic and cultural diversity that already exists in our classrooms, students are accustomed to variations in grouping, timing, teachers, materials, and noise levels. Even in classrooms without students who have an identified disability, varied activity, movement, and unexpected interruptions are a regular part of every school day—as described in the following section.

TIPS FROM AN INCLUSIVE EDUCATOR:
Setting Up an Inclusive Classroom Space

We played a lot of class games during the first month of school while I tried to establish routines and figure out how I was going to teach all four grades in the same room. I could see that the students much preferred to be treated as a whole class instead of as separate groups. Within their broad range of social and emotional development, I emphasized social skills and appropriate behavior every day. Without any outside behavior support for the classroom, embedding social skill instruction served as a proactive classroom management technique. Our classroom routines gradually evolved.

To meet the educational needs of the students, I had to create classroom spaces that appealed to and suited students in four different grades. I separated the classroom into learning centers where students could go to work on curriculum-related activities. There was a science area, a reading and writing space, an art corner, and a dramatic play center. At each center, there were different types of leveled materials for students of different ages and abilities. Fortunately, having the only primary class in the school came with some unique perks—I had all the supplies and resources I could want! I had different-sized desks to configure, books that were of varying levels of content, learning materials that suited different developmental stages, and four different types of notebooks for the students to write in. I had to have notebooks that were blank for my emerging writers, interlined journals for the students learning to print, double-spaced books for the students who were beginning writers, and single-spaced loose-leaf paper for the students who were skilled writers. I even had different types of writing tools available. There were large pencils and crayons for the kindergarten students who were developing their fine motor skills as well as markers and pencil crayons for the older students.

My approach to teaching so many different ability levels involved the basic principles of universal design for learning. I had an overarching theme that provided an umbrella for all our activities across the curriculum. For example, one month, our theme was "Bears"; another month, we studied Australia. Within those themes, I created core lessons that I taught the group. I used pictures, vocabulary cards, and demonstrations to reach nonreaders and maintain interest. Then, I provided follow-up activities based on the students' ability levels and interests. At times, I felt like the ringmaster of a three-ring circus! However, when I stopped and looked around at the buzzing hive of activity in the room, I was happy to see that the students were engaged in learning. Students were at different developmental levels and had a wide range of individual needs—but all had access to content within the same core academic subjects, addressing the same themes. Here are some ways to differentiate the curriculum and teach various levels of learners:

- Provide different levels of reading material.

- Simplify lessons by breaking down the concepts.

- Extend thinking by building on concepts.

- Group and instruct students based on ability level.

- Use charts and/or visuals to convey meaning.

- Demonstrate lesson concepts.

- Provide hands-on learning activities.

- Vary the length of time allotted to complete a lesson.

- Provide opportunities for large- and small-group work.

- Give students the opportunity to mentor one another.

- Reduce the number of questions.

- Ask students to complete only a portion of the assignment.

- Encourage students to represent their learning in different ways (e.g., presentations, computer or hand-made graphics, models, displays).

- Give students open-ended projects.

For more on this variation in student expression, see the discussion of UDL in the next section.

WAYS TO MAKE CLASSROOM INSTRUCTION INCLUSIVE

Inclusive education requires that teachers attempt to reach and teach all learners in the classroom. Teachers can begin by delivering lessons that give students various modalities for learning. Based on the science of brain development, *UDL* is an instructional framework that teachers can use to plan lessons. When more intense intervention is required, *multi-tiered systems of support (MTSS)* and curriculum adaptations in the form of *accommodations* can be used.

In this chapter, we will discuss the process of including all students in the curriculum at the school and classroom level. The chapter describes each of the different types of inclusive instruction that teachers can use: UDL, MTSS, and accommodations. (Chapters 5 and 6 will explore how the curriculum can be further adapted through modifications.) By delivering an inclusive, instructional framework of strategies known as UDL, most students will be able to access the curriculum and achieve the learning goals. However, in an inclusive class of students with various skill levels, some students will require more intentional support to access content. Therefore, we will also look at ways we can make the curriculum more accessible for students through adaptations in the form of accommodations. These accommodations can be provided within the research-based model known as MTSS. In MTSS, schools can provide an inclusive instructional framework of support based on the individual student's degree of need.

Universal Design for Learning

Universal design is a concept that has been applied to the environment around us for decades. It refers to the barrier-free design of products and buildings, which gives all people access to the greatest extent possible. Educators, with similar goals, have used this principle in daily instruction and called it *universal design for learning* or UDL. Within UDL, teachers reject the one-size-fits-all style of lesson delivery to give students flexible ways of accessing, engaging in, and demonstrating learning. Backed by research, "UDL provides a blueprint for creating instructional goals, methods, materials, and assessments that work for everyone—not a single, one-size-fits-all solution but rather flexible approaches that can be customized and adjusted for individual needs" (CAST National Center on Universal Design for Learning, 2016).

With UDL, teachers provide lessons and activities such as cooperative learning, differentiated instruction, and performance-based assessment. More specifically, teachers create lessons and activities that incorporate the following:

- **Multiple means of representation–**Information and content are presented in various ways, such as through visual, audio, and tactile materials.

- **Multiple means of action and expression–**Students can demonstrate their understanding of the material in numerous ways, such as written, spoken, artistic, or digital presentation.

- **Multiple means of engagement–**Teachers provide different ways for the student to engage and remain motivated during the lesson. For example, teachers can use inquiry-based projects, self-assessment, and learning software.

UDL can be beneficial to all learners, of all abilities and grades, including those who are working above or below grade level. It prompts teachers to plan ahead with their students' skills and needs in mind. When instruction is effectively delivered, students are interested in learning, have a deeper understanding of content, and achieve higher levels of success.

For example, suppose a Grade 3 teacher wants to give an introductory lesson on rocks. To motivate the students and activate prior knowledge, she begins the lesson with a story about rocks. After the story, she introduces several rock types and charts their characteristics on the whiteboard. The class discusses the differences. The teacher then creates small groups of students and gives each group samples of the three different types of rocks. She asks students to observe the rocks under a magnifying glass and to note color, size, interesting features, and weight. The students record their observations in a notebook. After the students have had time to record their observations, she brings the class back together and they take turns sharing their findings.

In this lesson, the teacher used multiple means of representation to present concepts through the use of a story and concrete objects. By charting rock characteristics, engaging in discussion, and taking observation notes, the students use multiple means of action and expression. Finally, the observation of the rock types and the class discussion are multiple ways to engage the students and make the lesson come to life.

UDL provides all students with access to the curriculum at the classroom level; if more direct, focused instruction is required, then support can be found in the school-based MTSS. This support system is established and maintained by school personnel (such as the learning resource teachers, therapists, and speech-language pathologists) to ensure that students with extra learning needs receive a level of instructional support appropriate to their needs.

Multi-Tiered Systems of Support

Many schools use an MTSS framework to facilitate academic and behavioral success for students. MTSS is a schoolwide approach to delivering specialized instruction and extra learning services to all students, including students with disabilities. MTSS is a continuum of systemwide support for students that extends beyond the classroom when required. It is based on a hierarchy of tiers ranging from low levels of support to higher, more intense levels. A common term used to describe the transition of services among the three tiers is *response to intervention (RTI)*. Here is a general description of services within the three tiers (Shapiro, n.d.):

- **Tier I**–the level of support provided to the majority of students within the general education classroom; at Tier I, all students receive high-quality instruction and appropriate support within a rigorous curriculum.

- **Tier II**–the level of increased support provided to the smaller segment of the student population that needs supplemental instruction beyond what teachers are already providing within the general curriculum. This support may be provided to students in small groups or one to one.

- **Tier III**–the most intensive level of support, which is provided to an even smaller segment of the student population that has more significant educational needs. This support is often provided through special education services and interventions tailored to the individual student's needs, and it typically involves more frequent progress monitoring than that provided for students at Tiers I and II.

Figure 4.1 depicts an MTSS. The academic and behavior supports at the base of the triangle are applied to all students and become gradually more intensive as the triangle narrows at the top, where it represents the supports provided to smaller numbers of students. The overall goal of using this model of service delivery is to provide a proactive, comprehensive approach to improving student learning as well as social and emotional outcomes.

A student can move in and out of levels or tiers depending on his or her needs at the time. MTSS begins with the premise that most students will make academic and behavioral gains by receiving standards-based instruction using highly effective teaching methods such as UDL. As mentioned previously, scaffolding, explicit instruction, differentiated activities, cooperative learning, and assistive technology facilitate learning within the UDL framework. Through the regular monitoring of both academic and behavioral performance, all students in the school receive support. Whether it is through effective daily instruction or positive classroom management programs, school staff ensure that every child's progress is monitored regularly. If a child is struggling to meet or maintain the expected academic and behavioral standards of his or her age group, then the child will receive targeted support for specific needs. This can happen in several different ways depending on the type and availability of support staff in the school, although it typically involves small-group instruction within the class or a resource room. If the child is still not meeting expectations, then he or she will be given intense, frequent instruction in a small-group or one-to-one format. A learning specialist typically delivers the more intense forms of support.

Students at any of the three tiers described previously may also need accommodations for learning; this applies to students with and without disabilities. Typical accommodations are described in the next section.

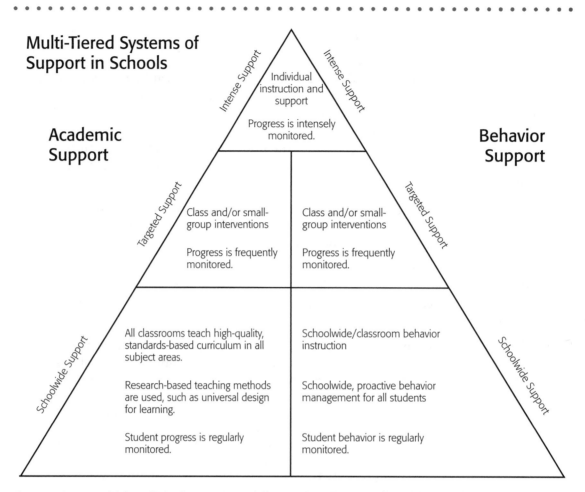

Multi-Tiered Systems of
Support in Schools

Academic
Support

Behavior
Support

Intense Support / Intense Support

Individual
instruction and
support

Progress is intensely
monitored.

Targeted Support / Targeted Support

Class and/or small-
group interventions

Progress is frequently
monitored.

Class and/or small-
group interventions

Progress is frequently
monitored.

Schoolwide Support / Schoolwide Support

All classrooms teach high-quality,
standards-based curriculum in all
subject areas.

Research-based teaching methods
are used, such as universal design
for learning.

Student progress is regularly
monitored.

Schoolwide/classroom behavior
instruction

Schoolwide, proactive behavior
management for all students

Student behavior is regularly
monitored.

Figure 4.1.   An example of a multi-tiered system of support that is used in inclusive schools. At the base of the triangle are the academic and behavior supports that are given to all students in the school. The supports become increasingly intensive in response to the higher needs of some students.

Accommodations for Learning

A student who works at or below grade level may require extra learning support through accommodations. Accommodations are pathways to the curriculum. They do not alter or change the objectives of a lesson, nor do they change the level of difficulty of a lesson.

Regardless of cognitive functioning, students can have physical, social, emotional, or neurological issues that prevent them from accessing the curriculum. For example, a student may have arthritis that makes writing difficult, have a hard time hearing when the teacher speaks, or have trouble sustaining attention during a lesson. These issues are chronic conditions that are barriers to learning. Whether or not the student qualifies for an IEP (as mentioned previously, to qualify for an IEP in the United States one must fall under certain categories of disabilities and require specialized instruction), the school is still required to support the student's education. Reducing the complexity of the content is not necessary in these situations because the student is able to understand the content; they just can't get to it in the first place. Therefore, supports, called *accommodations,* are provided to make the curriculum accessible.

Accommodations can be as informal as moving a student away from a distraction. Or, they can be as formal as providing a child with writing issues an assistive device that has speech-to-text software. When a child requires ongoing accommodations to successfully access the curriculum, a formal record is made in the student's IEP. If the student does not have an IEP, then a 504 plan is drafted. A 504 plan is a requirement of the Rehabilitation Act of 1973 (PL 93-112) and the Americans with Disabilities Act (ADA) of 1990 (PL 101-336), which mandates that people with disabilities must not be excluded from participating in federally funded programs and/or activities. This includes elementary, secondary, and postsecondary education.

Curriculum accommodations are not designed to give students with learning differences an advantage over their peers. Rather, these strategies or tools help provide access to curriculum that might not otherwise be available. Consider the example of a student who has a hearing impairment that prevents her from hearing the class lesson. The student, intellectually capable and motivated, does not receive the same information as her peers due to a physical limitation. Thus, the student does not have equal access to class material. If the student is given a hearing device, which enables hearing, the student can subsequently hear the lesson. Such support does not boost this child's achievement but rather enables her to participate fully in the same classwork as her peers.

There are dozens of such accommodations that can be made to address a range of learning needs. Here are some examples of accommodations at the school level, the classroom level, the curriculum level, and the individual level:

School

- Alternate room for tests, quiet time, work
- Big buddy
- Peer supports
- Visual reminders
- Morning announcements
- Digital announcements
- Alternate test schedule

Classroom

- Daily routine
- Suitable seating
- Visual reminders
- Hand signals
- Prompts and cues
- Audio support
- Various types of lighting
- Noise reduction
- Sensory reduction

Curriculum

- Speech-to-text software
- Color coordination of folders and materials

- Colored overlays for reading
- Highlighter pens
- Chunking of subject content
- Digital content
- Outlines of lesson material
- Calculator
- Photo of assignments and/or homework board
- Reduction of assignment

Student

- Checklists
- Timers
- Extended test-taking time
- Large print
- Various options for representation
- Extra set of books at home
- Peer helper
- Audio recorder
- Frequent breaks

Bear in mind that these accommodations are distinct from adaptations in the form of curriculum *modifications*. Curriculum modifications are created for students who work below grade level and make it possible for them to learn the same high-quality content. The concept of modification will be discussed at greater length in Chapter 5.

CONCLUSION

Instructional strategies and accommodations for learning can be made to help all students, of all abilities, access the curriculum. Just like their typically developing peers, students who have disabilities benefit from high-quality instructional strategies to understand curriculum. Instruction in the form of UDL presents information in a way that interests and motivates learners through multiple means of representation, expression, and engagement. When a student does not understand the concepts, however, a more intensive form of support is required; schools can provide this support within the MTSS framework, in which all students have access to high-quality instruction within the general curriculum (Tier I), and those students who need more intensive supports receive these supports at the Tier II or Tier III level as appropriate. Students with disabilities (like some of their peers) may also need curriculum accommodations to help them connect with material so that learning can take place. Chapter 5 will introduce and discuss the concept of curriculum modifications that help students who work below grade level achieve academic success.

CHAPTER 5

. . . .

Making Curriculum Achievable Through Modifications

Inclusion in education requires support in school, the classroom, the instructional process, and curriculum content to ensure that all students have access to the full core curriculum. Think about what it is like to participate in an experience in a passive or partial way versus participating fully. What if your friends were playing video games and all you could do was watch? Or, imagine going to the movie theater and not being able to see the movie screen. Such is the case with school. When a student goes to school and only participates in select classes, the student is not fully participating.

Inclusive schools create MTSS to include all students in instruction across the curriculum. These supports ensure that students succeed in all areas of school. If a child struggles to meet or maintain academic or behavior standards for his or her grade level within the general framework of supports the school and classroom provide, then extra assistance is provided where appropriate. This assistance may involve small-group instruction with a learning support teacher or one-to-one tutoring.

Some students can achieve the standards set for their grade but are hindered by a chronic condition that interferes with their learning. They don't need extra time reviewing the classwork or receiving direct instruction from a learning support teacher. They require help getting to the material. These students receive accommodations to facilitate access.

So, let's return to the analogy of the moviegoer who cannot see the screen. We can offer accommodations such as a closer seat, a view that isn't blocked, or a pair of glasses. What if, however, the moviegoer has an ID? Using eyeglasses or switching seats will not change his or her ability to comprehend the storyline. So, do we prevent the moviegoer from seeing the movie because we feel that his or her understanding will be minimal? Let's think inclusively about the situation. We know we can provide some background information about the movie prior to viewing it. We know that the movie's sound and images will provide visual and auditory support for understanding. Also, we can offer intermittent explanation of the storyline. Therefore, the movie experience will be modified and hopefully enjoyed to the greatest extent possible. That sure beats staying at home!

Some students need only a few fairly simple changes, or accommodations, to access curriculum; others need more carefully thought out changes, or modifications. Accommodations can be used to facilitate access to content material in the general education classroom. However, if a student has cognitive challenges and cannot work at an age-appropriate grade level, then accommodations will not provide enough learning support. For these students, making the existing curriculum *accessible* is not an educationally appropriate goal; rather, the curriculum itself must be modified to make it *achievable* for the student. That is, the nature and purpose of the curriculum change are different because the student's needs are different.

Fortunately, changes, deletions, and substitutions to the curriculum can be made to make grade-level content suitable for a student with disabilities. These personalized forms of support go beyond typical accommodations and classroom interventions. Educators know these kinds of adaptations as *curriculum modifications*.

Chapter 6 will explore the concept of making the curriculum available to students who work below grade level. This process is known as *modifying curriculum*. I will describe the intent and process of making curriculum modifications and their relevance to inclusive education. In fact, they are so essential that without them, students who are working below grade level will continue to be marginalized and excluded from their seemingly inclusive classrooms.

TIPS FROM AN INCLUSIVE EDUCATOR:

Learning the Basics of Curriculum Modification

When I began teaching, the students in my class had very little supplemental teaching or learning support during my first year at the school. The learning assistance teacher and school counselor made visits as often as they could—once a week at most. An alternate class for full-day direct service or pullout support did not exist. Thankfully, as part of my preservice training, I had taken some courses in special education. I came up with a few ways to provide extra assistance when I could. I either addressed the student's individual issue during the lesson (embedded skill development), worked directly with the student once the lesson was over (one-to-one instruction), or set up peer tutoring groups.

Interestingly, despite the wide range of ages in the class and variety of activities going on, I was able to support students better than I initially thought, by keeping the following ideas in mind:

It is the classroom teacher's responsibility to teach ALL students. I can't stress enough how important it is for inclusive teachers to take responsibility for teaching all students in the classroom. There will be students who require extra learning support and/or special education services beyond the capacity of the classroom teacher, but those extra services do not and should never make up the student's entire education program.

Think about what the student can do. Remember that in a strength-based classroom, teachers see the child's strengths first.

Focus on ability level and not grade level. This was how I ensured that each student could learn and work on material that was appropriate to his or her learning needs. Having so many different grades in the class made it easy to accommodate different levels of learning.

Connect and collaborate with staff. Many of my best teaching ideas over the years have come from my colleagues. There is tremendous value in learning from the experience of others. One of my most memorable tips was a positive behavior management strategy that came from my friend's sister who was also a teacher. Essentially, I grouped the students and gave each group a color. I used the color names to organize student work, activities, lessons, and movement in the classroom. For example, when

I wanted the students to line up at the door, rather than have the whole class move toward the door at once, I would ask groups to line up by color.

Get creative. Think beyond modifying the paper-and-pencil work that is expected of students. Think of ways to appropriately incorporate technology, art, and/or tactile materials into the lesson.

WHAT ARE CURRICULUM MODIFICATIONS?

As a matter of course, I learned to work with students of various grade levels in my classroom and include them in every lesson. In fact, taking grade-level curriculum and modifying it for students who work below grade level is an essential task for inclusive educators in any type of classroom. Research findings indicate, "Curriculum modifications have been identified as critical if students with disabilities are to achieve access to and make progress in the general education curriculum" (Lee, Wehmeyer, Soukup, & Palmer, 2010, p. 214). Unlike accommodations, which make curriculum *accessible,* modifications make curriculum *achievable.*

Interestingly, there is no official definition of the term *curriculum modification.* It is widely accepted in the education community that curriculum modifications involve combinations of altered content, conceptual difficulty, educational goals, and instructional method (Hall, Vue, Koga, & Silva, 2004). For example:

- **Altering content** means to teach the student content that is related to the grade-level curriculum but is more suited to the student's educational needs. For example, a student on a modified program in a fifth-grade class might learn how plants grow by planting an actual seed and observing its growth over time rather than learning about the plant's cellular functions.

- **Altering conceptual difficulty** means to simplify the concept to a level of student understanding. One of my favorite strategies was to create tiers of work in a student activity. Each tier was a variation in the level of difficulty in the learning outcomes. For example, I would deliver a lesson to the whole group. After the lesson, I gave all the students the same follow-up activity. However, different learning outcomes were expected from each grade level. For instance, after a story, I would expect students who worked at the kindergarten level to draw a picture about the story and tell me about it. Students at the first- and second-grade level would write a few sentences, whereas students working at the third-grade level would write a paragraph. In this way, all children participated in very similar basic lesson activities—reading or listening to the story and retelling it—but each child was expected to understand the story, and retell it, at a conceptual level appropriate to that child's developmental level. Streamlining the lesson and leveling the follow-up activity kept all my students involved and able to participate—unless, of course, a kindergarten student decided it was naptime.

- **Altering the educational goals** means to change the learning expectations of the lesson. For example, a teacher can modify a math sheet on fractions to create a math sheet on addition by having the student add the numerator and denominator of the fraction.

- **Altering the instructional method** means to provide the student with disabilities an alternate and better-suited form of instruction. For example, the teacher might ask the class to read a passage and answer 10 related questions. However, the activity is recreated in cloze format (key words are left out of the passage) for the student on a modified program.

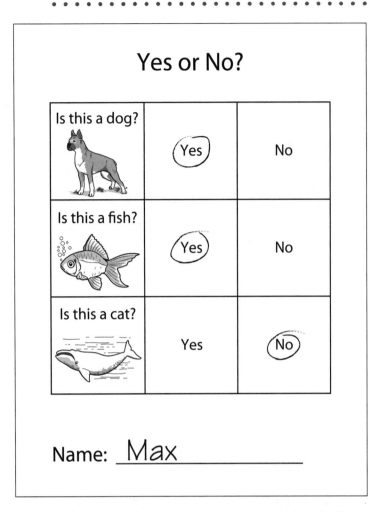

Figure 5.1. Example of a science modification for a student in fourth grade. The student, who works below grade level, is working on his ability to accurately identify animals at the same time his class learns the concept of food chains.

A modification is versatile, used throughout all grades, and can be applied to any aspect of the curriculum. Figure 5.1 is an example of a science modification for a student who works below grade level in a fourth-grade class. Both the student and his classmates are learning about living things and their environment. While the class learns the concept of food chains, the student works on his recognition and recall skills by identifying animals. In this case, it is the *conceptual difficulty* of the curriculum that has been altered; the concepts the student learns are related to those in the general curriculum but are appropriate to his level. The *educational goals* of the lesson have also been altered to better suit the student's learning needs. Finally, the *instructional method* has also changed. The student demonstrates his understanding of the lesson through yes/no questions while the class is working with grade-level text.

Another example of a modified lesson can be seen in Figure 5.2. This example is a fifth-grade language arts modification. Students in the class are expected to learn 20 spelling words per week. The student on the modified language arts program is expected to learn five words per week. She uses the same spelling list as her peers. However, the conceptual difficulty of the words is altered. Less-complex words are used and can be found embedded within the original class list. Just like her peers, though, she must read the words and reprint them. Thus, in this example, the *conceptual difficulty* and *educational goals* of the lesson have changed.

WHY MODIFY?

Switlick states that the purpose of modifying curriculum is "to enable an individual to compensate for intellectual, physical, or behavioral challenges" and to create learning environments that "allow the individual to use existing skill repertoires while promoting the acquisition of new skills and knowledge" (1997, p. 236). In countries such as the United States, providing modifications to curriculum is a component of FAPE, which is required by the IDEA 2004 and state law. A November 2015 guidance letter from the U.S. Department of

Education includes a statement about the purpose of curriculum modifications. It reads:

> In a situation where a child is performing significantly below the level of the grade in which the child is enrolled, an IEP Team should determine annual goals that are ambitious but achievable. In other words, the annual goals need not necessarily result in the child's reaching grade-level within the year covered by the IEP, but the goals should be sufficiently ambitious to help close the gap. The IEP must also include the specialized instruction to address the unique needs of the child that result from the child's disability necessary to ensure access of the child to the general curriculum, so that the child can meet the State academic content standards that apply to all children in the State. (Yudin & Musgrove, 2015, p. 7)

Judging from the statistics I mentioned at the beginning of this book, which stated that only 16% of students with IDs are included in the general education classroom for more than 80% of the day, we can conclude that special education teachers largely take responsibility for curriculum modifications. A teacher who is prepared and equipped with the skills to modify curriculum within the general education classroom can help improve those statistics.

Name: Olivia   Date: 1/26/18

Grade 5 Spelling Practice

Copy the following words.

ser**vant**	serv<u>ant</u>
im**port**ant	im<u>port</u>ant
exc**it**able	exc<u>it</u>able
ple**as**ant	ple<u>as</u>ant
partici**pant**	partici<u>pant</u>

Figure 5.2. Example of a language arts modification for a student in fifth grade. The student works at a Grade 1 level and can recognize simple words. The teacher creates a modified spelling list from the original class.

There is overwhelming research to support the benefits of modifying curriculum and the impact it has on student attitudes, self-concept, and school performance. Salisbury et al. (1994) found that when curriculum was modified for students with mild to profound needs, the students were successfully included during physical, social, and instructional time. Furthermore, Lee and colleagues (2010) observed high school students with disabilities during instruction in the core subjects. They noticed that when curriculum modifications were given, students were engaged in more academic-related responses and had fewer disruptive behaviors, and teachers spent less time managing class activities. Certainly, curriculum modifications can be the difference between learning in a special education classroom and learning in a general education classroom.

It's important to mention that the student is not missing out by having modified goals. Rather, the modified goals fall within the student's zone of proximal development. The *zone of proximal development* is a well-known education concept developed by Lev Vygotsky. He defines it as "the distance between the actual developmental level as determined by independent problem solving and the level of potential development as determined through problem-solving under adult guidance, or in collaboration with more capable peers"

(Vygotsky, 1978, p. 86). Put more simply, this is the difference between what a student can do independently and what a student needs targeted instruction to learn to do. For instance, a child learning to play guitar may be able to hold the guitar, fret the strings with one hand, and strum with the other hand. Nevertheless, she may struggle to coordinate these motions well enough to play a chord clearly and may be able to do so only when a teacher is physically assisting her. The child has the potential to learn to play chords and, eventually, songs. To realize this potential, however, she needs a teacher's guidance and must progress gradually by learning increasingly challenging skills. In an education setting, working with students' zone of proximal development means giving them tasks that are achievable but will stretch their learning and thinking skills. The modifications shown in Figures 5.1 and 5.2 and discussed previously are just two example of such tasks.

HOW ARE CURRICULUM MODIFICATIONS MADE?

Modifications are not used lightly. Curriculum modifications can have an impact on a student's graduation status and eligibility for postsecondary programs. Thus, determining the need for curriculum modifications is a formal process that involves school personnel, the student's family, and in most cases, the student. Curriculum modifications are always documented in the IEP. Here is a general overview of the steps that must be taken to create an IEP with curriculum modifications:

- **Child is struggling in school.** Either staff or parents bring the child's challenges and issues to the attention of the school.

- **Child is evaluated.** Specialized staff carry out evaluations on the child to identify any barriers to learning.

- **Child's eligibility is determined.** In accordance with IDEA 2004, it is decided whether the child has a disability that is eligible for special education services.

- **IEP meeting is arranged.** A meeting is scheduled among the student's parents or guardians, school staff, and any other support personnel to create the student's IEP.

- **IEP is written.** The IEP is drawn up with educational goals related to the student's academic, social, emotional, and physical needs. School districts often develop guidelines for developing IEPs so they best meet the needs of students. Naming **SMART goals** (goals that are **S**pecific, **M**easurable, **A**chievable, **R**ealistic, and **T**ime-bound [Doran, 1981; Ralabate, 2016]), identifying a means of achieving goals, establishing the assessment and reporting of goals, and naming the types of supports and services needed to achieve the goal are examples of issues that need to be discussed by the student's IEP team. Prioritizing an alignment of goals within a student's IEP and the grade-level curriculum is a common practice in inclusive education. For instance, if a student in eighth grade is working below grade level in science, his or her goals do not need to be eighth-grade science goals. Instead, they are IEP goals that can be worked on within the same theme or strand of science. School IEP teams work to create a balance of goals ranging from functional to academic. (Guidance on the formation of inclusive IEP goals can be found in the work of inclusion experts such as June Downing, Lou Brown, Martha Snell, and Rachel Janney. All have written extensively about the process of including students with disabilities in academic instruction.) Finally, the school and the student's family must be in agreement on the goals before the IEP can be implemented.

Program-at-a-Glance	
Student _Chase_	Date _September 2012_

IEP goals (in a few words)	IEP accommodations and modifications
Social-communication and self-management • Increase communication skills in group activities: make eye contact, face speaker, use relevant questions and answers. • Respond to and initiate positive interactions (e.g., greetings, requests) with peers. • Use self-control strategies with cues and support. **Functional skills and class participation** • Follow the class procedures from the teachers' cues. • Follow school routines: arrival, departure, lunch, and classroom jobs. **Math** • Read, write, and compare numbers 0–100. • Add and subtract to 50 using concrete objects. • Tell time to 15 minutes (analog, digital). • Use measurements: pounds, inches and feet, cups and quarts. • Identify and compare basic geometric figures. • Construct and interpret basic bar, picture, and line graphs. **Reading and language arts** • Answer "wh-" questions for fiction and nonfiction stories. • Read familiar stories and passages with fluency. • Read, write, or spell one-syllable words with beginning and ending consonants. • Write to communicate: three-sentence paragraph. • Collect topical information from print and online. **Science and social studies** • Locate and identify national and state capitols. • Identify contributions of famous Americans. • Investigate and understand magnets. • Investigate and understand relationships among organisms in aquatic and terrestrial food chains. • Learn three to four key vocabulary terms per unit, with an emphasis on comparison, safety, problem solving, and measurement. • Conduct investigations (predict, observe, conclude; cause and effect).	• Special education support instruction for academics, daily routines, transitions, and social-communication • Modified curriculum • Weekly curricular and instructional adaptations by special education and general education teachers • Science and social studies texts read aloud or with computer text reader • Math, science, and social studies tests read aloud • Additional scheduled movement breaks • Daily home–school communication log • Educational team familiar with and uses positive behavior interventions and supports (PBIS) plan • Visual daily schedule • Visual organizer and checklists for task steps of multistep activities and investigations **Behavior and other support needs** • Peer support network (e.g., lunch bunch) • Clear time limits and beginnings and endings to activities and assignments • See PBIS plan; share key strategies with all relevant teachers and staff **Comments and other special needs** • Core team meetings approximately every other week; whole team meetings approximately monthly

Figure 5.3. Program-at-a-Glance for Chase, a fourth-grade student. (Key: IEP, individualized education program.) (From Janney, R., & Snell, M.E. [2013]. *Modifying schoolwork* [3rd ed., p. 93]. Baltimore, MD: Paul H. Brookes Publishing Co. Reprinted by permission.)

• **Services are delivered.** The student receives services (e.g., therapies, behavior plans, accommodations, curriculum modifications) when all parties agree on the goals and delivery of the student's IEP. The presence of curriculum modifications in a student's education program can have long-term effects on the student's opportunities beyond high school. Identifying achievable curriculum goals for a student who works below grade level requires the collaborative effort of the special education teacher, the classroom teacher, support personnel, and family.

• **Progress is assessed and reported.** The student's progress in relation to his or her IEP goals is measured and reported to stakeholders. Once the IEP has been developed and the modified goals identified, the classroom teacher receives a copy. It's a good idea for teachers to also have an at-a-glance page that they can keep on hand while planning class lessons. Figure 5.3 is an example of a program-at-a-glance. It gives the reader essential information about the student's educational goals. When planning class lessons, the teacher identifies ways in which the student can participate while meeting the goals of his or her IEP.

Using Chase's goals to illustrate (from Figure 5.3), the teacher can ask Chase to work on his goal of recognizing numbers to 100 while his class works on writing the expanded form of numbers. Likewise, in science, Chase can learn plant vocabulary while the class learns about plants and sunlight. Figure 5.4 is an example of the modified science activity.

• **IEP is reevaluated at least once a year.** The IEP is revisited at least once a year to ensure that educational goals are appropriate and that the student is making progress.

All of these decisions about whether to modify curriculum and if so, how, take place within the larger context of creating an inclusive classroom environment. Meston and Cranston (2011) remind us that the goal of inclusive classrooms is to have all students working with similar curriculum content and related materials. To illustrate ways in which a student can participate in a class lesson with adaptations (both accommodations and modifications),

Name: Oria	Date:

Parts of a Flower

Read	Copy
Flower	Flower
Petal	Petal
Leaf	Leaf
Stem	Stem
Roots	Roots

Figure 5.4. Example of a modified science activity for Chase. Chase works on his IEP goal of learning key vocabulary while the class is assigned an activity on plants and sunlight.

Salisbury et al. (1994) developed a progression of five lesson formats that describe the most inclusive lesson format to the least inclusive. The most inclusive has the student with disabilities working on the same activity with the same objectives and materials as his or her classmates. No accommodations or modifications are required. If that level is not appropriate for the student with disabilities, the next level has the student working on the same activity with a modified objective and the same materials as his or her classmates. This is the most inclusive format for students who work below grade level. In Salisbury's et al.'s original progression, three more levels follow, with the activity, objective, and materials becoming increasingly different from the original lesson. However, within the past two decades, educational philosophy regarding disability inclusion has further evolved to emphasize the importance of the least dangerous assumption (Donellan, 1984)—that is, "in the absence of conclusive data educational decisions ought to be based on assumptions which, if incorrect, will have the least dangerous effect on the likelihood that students will be able to function independently as adults." In other words, as educators we cannot always gauge the true extent of students' abilities. To avoid potentially doing harm by assuming students to be less capable than they actually are, we must err on the side of assuming capability. Thus, even when students have severe disabilities, they should engage in the same classroom activities as peers if possible and, ideally, work with the same objective or a modified version thereof. Figure 5.5 is a chart outlining the first three (i.e., most inclusive) levels of inclusion identified by Salisbury et al. (1994). The level of inclusion at which a student works depends on the subject and the ability of the student. A student might work at grade level in math, yet need a modified language arts curriculum. Frequent progress monitoring keeps the teacher informed of what the student is capable of doing.

CONCLUSION

General education teachers, with little to no preservice training in special education (a predominant situation in the United States), can feel ill-equipped to create curriculum modifications for students who work below grade level. Special education teachers assist with planning, intervention, and support, but demanding caseloads can limit their time to plan

• •

Description and Illustration of the Curriculum Adaptation Process

---

Level 1. *Same Activity and Objective, Same Materials*

Goals and objectives from the student's IEP are able to be addressed within the regular curriculum/lessons. Goals and objectives will be no different from those of the student's peers and no adaptation is needed. If the student evidences a sensory impairment, access to the curriculum can be modified through the use of appropriate modifications (e.g., braille, hearing aid, sign).

(A) Kim participates in the rational-counting/numeral-writing activity using the same materials and under the same expectations for performance as her peers. No adaptations are required.

Level 2. *Same Activity Easier Step (Modified Objective), Same Materials*

At this level the student participates in the curriculum at a prerequisite level relative to his or her peers. That is, the activity remains the same, but the objectives for the student are different. Ways of responding may be adapted (e.g., listen rather than read, speak rather than write). Relative to the previous level, instruction at this stage is more individualized.

(A) Kim works on counting and writing numbers less than 5, while her classmates work on numbers up to 10.
(B) Kim works on only counting objects, and will blend the counting and writing processes at some future date.
(C) Kim listens to the teacher give the answer, then writes the correct number on the line under the picture.
(D) Kim counts out objects and tells peer how many (what number) to write on the answer sheet.

Level 3. *Same Activity, Different Objective and Materials*

At this point in the process, the activity the student is engaged in remains the same as his or her peers, but the objective and materials are changed to enable the student to remain an equal participant in the activity. The degree of individualization is greater at this level, yet the student remains included at the table or desks with his or her peers for instruction.

(A) Kim uses a template to trace numbers on a wide-lined piece of paper.
(B) Kim is asked to match her counting objects to the sample provided in plastic bins in front of her on the table.
(C) Kim traces numbers written in yellow highlighter.
(D) Kim counts out objects with a peer and glues items under the appropriate numeral.

Figure 5.5. Chart outlining the three most inclusive levels of inclusion. (Description and Illustration of the Curriculum Adaptation Process by Salisbury, C., Mangino, M., Petrigala, M., Rainforth, B., Syryca, S., & Palombaro, M. [1994]. Promoting the Instructional Inclusion of Young Children With Disabilities in the Primary Grades. *Journal of Early Intervention, 18*[3], Adapted and reprinted with permission.)

with the general education teacher. As a result, the student may not be included in any, or all, academic instruction within the class. As mentioned previously, general education teachers can facilitate inclusion and modify grade-level curriculum to meet the goals in a student's IEP. This chapter introduced a few core strategies for modifying curriculum: altering the content, conceptual difficulty, educational goals, and/or instructional method. More specific strategies for making modifications will be provided in Section II of this book.

Modifying Curriculum for Students Who Work Below Grade Level

. . . .

Research-Based Curriculum Modifications for Inclusion

My time spent teaching the primary class in a rural school in northern British Columbia was a unique experience. It dramatically altered my teaching practice and reshaped my philosophy of education. I had to think outside the box as I juggled curriculum, instruction, and activities. I had to find resources in the most unlikely places due to the limited support staff and learning materials. I remember the excitement I felt when I discovered that the school bus driver, who doubled as the first-aid attendant and security officer, was also willing to teach a science lesson or two. I had to change my teaching style to accommodate the kindergarten student who needed help tying shoes and the third grader who was learning multiplication. Finally, I learned how to include students in class instruction when I simply didn't think it was possible.

The lessons I learned in my first job, well over 20 years ago now, have continued to guide my practice in education and my commitment to advocating for inclusive education. When I moved on to subsequent teaching positions, I had confidence in my ability to reach diverse learners in the general education classroom. From my experiences, I can tell you with certainty that we all benefit from classrooms rich in diversity. Most important, schools, classrooms, and curriculum can come together to support students of all levels and abilities. Above all, inclusive education *can* and *does* happen.

MODIFICATIONS: DIFFERENT WAYS TO MAKE THE SAME CURRICULUM ACHIEVABLE

Traditionally, students who worked below grade level were denied access to their age-appropriate general education classroom. Most people believed that a more appropriate setting was the special education classroom, where these students could receive specialized services in a segregated environment. However, in this environment, the student spent little time interacting with his or her peers. Students with disabilities have a right to access the same opportunities and curriculum as their peers. Also, research has proven that both groups make academic and social gains when students have equal access to the same curriculum. The overwhelming benefits of inclusive education are too significant to be dismissed, and more students with disabilities should have the opportunity to learn in general education classrooms. Providing school supports, classroom instructional supports, and curriculum supports paves the way to inclusion. However, it is the process of modifying curriculum that gives students who work below grade level a full, authentic education.

This process has typically been the responsibility of the special education teacher and support personnel. Given the lack of training, classroom teachers who do want to modify curriculum often rely on the expertise of the special education teacher. However, the reality of schedules, caseloads, and the administrative demands of special education teachers limits planning time. Classroom teachers need the knowledge and strategies to feel competent enough to include learners who work below grade level.

This chapter will outline the *research that proves these strategies yield positive outcomes*. Also, there are suggestions for ways in which teachers can easily implement the strategies in daily lessons. Most of these strategies will be familiar to teachers, but it is my goal to show how to use them to teach your students who work below grade level.

MAINTAINING HIGH STANDARDS WHILE MODIFYING CURRICULUM

Do we expect students who are typically developing to learn the bare minimum? No. Through a 2009 federal initiative called the Common Core State Standards (CCSS), high-quality academic standards for mathematics and English language arts have been set for the majority of American students. Established in recognition of the need to provide all students with a quality education, the CCSS are learning goals that students are expected to meet by the end of each grade level. CCSS are research-based, aligned with college and career expectations, and based on rigorous content that encourages students to develop and use their higher order thinking skills. More specifically,

> The Common Core is informed by the highest, most effective standards from states across the United States and countries around the world. The standards define the knowledge and skills students should gain throughout their K-12 education in order to graduate high school prepared to succeed in entry-level careers, introductory academic college courses, and workforce training programs. (National Governors Association Center for Best Practices and the Council of Chief State School Officers, 2010)

Moreover, the CCSS apply to all students, including students with disabilities. The CCSS's Application to Students with Disabilities section states, "These common standards provide an historic opportunity to improve access to rigorous academic content standards for students with disabilities" (Common Core State Standards Initiative, n.d.). To facilitate access to the content and standards of Common Core, students with disabilities are legally entitled to the appropriate supports, related services, trained personnel, and an Individual Education Program where necessary (National Governors Association Center for Best Practices and the Council of Chief State School Officers, 2010).

Using the CCSS Initiative as an example, it is clear that our education mandate is to promote a culture of high expectations for *all* students and not just a select group. As McNulty and Gloeckler noted, "Not every student with disabilities will meet academic standards, but that is not a reason to stop providing support to help them achieve at high levels of learning" (2014, p. 7). Thus, educators must carefully design curriculum modifications to help students with disabilities achieve high levels of learning.

INSTRUCTIONAL STRATEGIES THAT MODIFY CURRICULUM

When educators modify curriculum, they are teaching students concepts that are within their range of abilities and development. Although the learning standards may be at a different grade level than those of same-age peers, educators still need to take the time to use high-quality content. Students with disabilities can be challenged to think deeper and use higher level thinking skills, with appropriate supports as needed.

Teachers can use instructional strategies to shape and modify curriculum while maintaining high standards for learning. These strategies are derived from research and evidence to promote a deeper understanding of the content and facilitate the higher order thinking skills that are expected of students. Keep in mind, it is not only the learning outcome of the strategy that creates quality education. There is tremendous value in the process in which those lessons are learned. In the following section, I explain how the modification strategies chosen for this book to develop skills have both immediate and far-reaching benefits for students with disabilities.

Strategies That Encourage Deeper Learning: Productive Struggle

When teachers see students struggle to learn new concepts, instinct is to intervene immediately. Usually, the teacher re-explains the lesson, presents the concept in an alternate format, and even sometimes goes so far as to solve the problem for the student. Teachers are trained to help students succeed and learn the new material. What if, however, students can be far more successful when we don't step in right away to help out? Research suggests that letting students work through an activity, try different methods of problem solving, and persist despite uncertainty is actually an important part of learning.

For decades, education experts have documented the benefits of *productive struggle* in education. Productive struggle as an inherent part of learning has been recognized and written about as early as 1910, which is when education reformer John Dewey "described learning as beginning with a dilemma – an uncertainty about how to proceed. Struggling to work through uncertainty and ambiguity to discover a solution was, for Dewey, essential to meaningful learning" (Ermeling, Hiebert, & Gallimore, 2015). Meanwhile, psychologist Jean Piaget (1960) tells us that learners develop disequilibrium as they struggle to master new material. During this struggle, their disequilibrium is restructured toward understanding. However, it is important to mention that the teacher needs to be attentive to the progress a student makes as he or she moves through a challenging activity. Productive struggle can stop being productive once the student becomes frustrated, angry, or upset.

Through productive struggle, students are encouraged to stretch their thinking, persist, and use problem-solving skills. Most recently, the concept of applying productive struggle to learning mathematics has been the focus of education researchers. In 2014, researcher Hiroko Kawaguchi Warshauer examined periods of time when students appeared to struggle to learn a concept in their middle school math class. In the case study, Warshauer analyzed 186 episodes of students engaged in a task that required higher level cognitive thinking skills. Using a framework to describe the episode of struggle from start to finish, Warshauer looked at the data and drew several implications for students and teachers. The case study suggested that there is a productive role of student struggle in learning and understanding. Furthermore, rather than avoid or prevent, teachers can incorporate productive struggle in lessons to help students develop a deeper understanding of new concepts. The instructional strategies in this book can provide numerous opportunities for students to engage in this very important aspect of learning.

Strategies That Can Extend Thinking

Educators use strategies to expand students' thinking skills—but not all thinking skills are equal. A question such as *Is the grass green?* can prompt a much different response from most students than *What would have to happen to make the grass green?* The first question elicits a yes/no answer, whereas the second one requires the student to give a detailed, scientific response. In both cases, the student is using thinking skills to answer the question. With the goal of creating 21st-century learners, educators expect that all students will learn and develop the ability to use more complex thinking skills over the course of their school years. These skills are known as higher order thinking skills.

Higher order thinking skills can be defined as those that help us learn and use knowledge and reason, and think before deciding what to believe or do, as well as solve problems to reach a desired outcome (Brookhart, 2010). In 2001, Harold Wenglinsky showed that learning higher order thinking skills is essential to student achievement. However, teaching a variety of thinking skills (particularly thinking skills that are more complex) has traditionally been reserved for high-achieving students. Taylor and MacKenney wrote, "This tactic assumes that students with disabilities cannot benefit from instruction in reasoning until basic skills are mastered" (2008, p. 139). However, research shows that students with disabilities benefit from learning higher order thinking skills (Carnine, 1991; Jalloul & EL-Daou, 2016; Lombardi & Savage, 1994; Means & Knapp, 1991; Zohar & Dori, 2003). Students make gains in academic achievement and can apply their knowledge to solve problems and develop new ideas. Moreover, teaching higher order thinking skills fosters self-esteem and creates enthusiasm for learning (Campbell & Chastain-Bogy, 1996). Teaching these skills to all students, including students with disabilities, is also a provision of the Every Student Succeeds Act of 2015 (Cook-Harvey et al., 2016).

For decades, educators have sought to identify and categorize thinking skills; a particularly well-known example of this is Bloom's taxonomy, developed in 1956. Bloom's taxonomy outlined a hierarchy of thinking skills, from *lower level skills* (e.g., recognition, recall) to higher level skills (e.g., synthesis, evaluation). In this taxonomy, each skill was built upon the one preceding it, and the lower levels of the taxonomy were less valued than the higher ones. In 2007, in response to new research and theories about thinking and learning, educational researchers Robert Marzano and John Kendall published a revised version of the taxonomy in their book, *The New Taxonomy of Educational Objectives.*

Marzano and Kendall's new taxonomy is based on a well-established psychological theory that thinking skills do not need to be taught in order because even the most complex level of processing can be learned and performed with little or no effort when one is familiar with the task (Marzano & Kendall, 2007). For example, when my son was 4 years old, he was passionate about dinosaurs. He would look at the same dinosaur books over and over again. Even though he hadn't learned to read and write most basic sight words yet, he was able to identify and sight-read the complicated scientific names of more than a dozen prehistoric reptiles. His word recognition skills, and his learning of other skills involved in the complex act of reading, developed at different rates that depended in part upon his interests, motivation, and familiarity with the topic. The new taxonomy recognizes that our level of thinking depends on our interest in the topic and executive function skills (i.e., setting a goal to learn specific information). Thus, Marzano and Kendall's new taxonomy is a two-dimensional one that names three different types of knowledge and the systems of processing that are applied to each knowledge domain (see Figure 6.1). Within the cognitive system is where a hierarchal list of thinking skills makes up the basis of the taxonomy. For a more detailed explanation of the taxonomy, please refer to Marzano and Kendall (2007).

Marzano and Kendall (2008) stated that the taxonomy can be used in several ways. For this book's purposes, it will be used as a framework for teaching different types of thinking skills. However, educators are warned against teaching a thinking skills curriculum only to high-achieving students. Rather, the curriculum should be accessible to all learners of all ability levels. In addition, the thinking skills should not be taught in a continuum from lower to higher order skills, with students mastering one level before moving on to the next. Thinking skills should be taught within the context of the lesson and when appropriate (National Research Council, 1987).

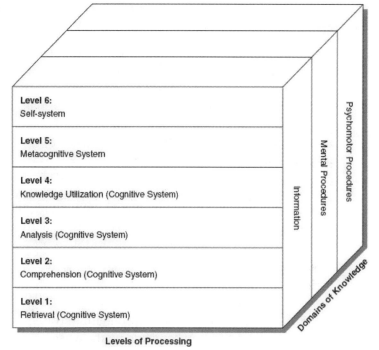

Figure 6.1. The new taxonomy. (From Marzano, R., & Kendall, J. [2008]. *Designing and assessing educational objectives: Applying the new taxonomy*, p. 2. Thousand Oaks, CA: Corwin Press. Reprinted with permission.)

Marzano and Kendall (2008) encouraged teachers to use the taxonomy as a foundation for curriculum design and instruction. Through the use of the taxonomy, teachers can plan lessons that will give students an opportunity to use different types of thinking skills (see Figure 6.1). Some lessons encourage students to list, name, or recall information. Other lessons have students researching their favorite animal to create a report for the class—a more complex task involving comprehension skills and, potentially, analysis of new information and the application of acquired knowledge to complex questions or situations.

The modification strategies in this book prompt a range of learning activities that facilitate the different types of thinking skills seen in Marzano and Kendall's (2007) taxonomy: **retrieval, comprehension, analysis,** and **knowledge utilization.** As with the taxonomy, the strategies are grouped according to the different types of cognitive processing, as follows:

1. **Retrieval strategies**–These strategies encourage students to process information through recognition, recall, and execution.

2. **Comprehension strategies**–These strategies require students to use information to develop and demonstrate an understanding of new content.

3. **Analysis strategies**–The strategies within this group require students to analyze and draw conclusions about new information through activities such as classifying, matching, and generalizing.

4. **Knowledge utilization strategies**–This group of strategies has students applying their knowledge to work through complex cognitive tasks such as generating and testing hypotheses.

HOW TO USE THE STRATEGIES

Some of the strategies presented in Chapter 7 will seem familiar to most educators. What is new, however, are the ways you can use these strategies to modify curriculum for students for whom the grade-level curriculum is not developmentally appropriate. As mentioned previously, the strategies are grouped according to the four levels of thinking skills. Each strategy comes with a description, learning outcomes, classroom activities with which the strategy can be used, directions for use, and tips for further interventions and/or extensions of the activity. I also provide an example of student work and the context for this work; that is, how the work the student did relates to the grade-level curriculum and/or the student's IEP goals.

As you select curriculum modification strategies for use in your own classroom, it will be up to you to determine what level of thinking strategy is appropriate for a particular student. Also, remember that the strategies do not have to all be pencil-and-paper work. These strategies can be taken off the page and used with assistive technology and various forms of media. Finally, you can use this resource in the following ways:

- Keep a written record of other resources you find helpful when modifying content.

- Highlight parts of the strategy that worked or did not work.

- Copy and laminate the reproducible strategy forms available in Appendix B, so you can have them on hand and ready to use.

- Share the strategies with other teachers.

- Consider the philosophy, general principles, and specific strategies discussed in this book to be a springboard for new ideas and inspiration.

CONCLUSION

Modifying curriculum to include students who work below grade level has profound benefits. Students with disabilities can spend more time with their peers learning high-quality curriculum through research-based strategies. The strategies in Chapter 7 will give teachers the ability to feel competent and confident that they are providing educational experiences to help students achieve success. Appendix A provides a list of resources that you will find helpful in modifying curriculum and including all kinds of learners in your classroom.

CHAPTER 7

· · · · · · · · · · ·

The Strategies

The previous six chapters of this book have presented an overview of inclusion and the reasons why true inclusion must address the needs of *all* students. I have discussed ways you can work with fellow educators, school support staff, students, and community members to create inclusive school and classroom environments, and ways to make curriculum accessible through accommodations or alter it through modifications. Recall that curriculum modifications involve making substantial changes to content, conceptual difficulty, educational goals, instructional method, or any combination of these. In contrast to accommodations, which make the grade-level curriculum accessible, modifications make curriculum *possible and achievable* for students for whom the grade-level curriculum is not accessible even with supports.

Chapter 7 will present 40 specific strategies for curriculum modification, aligned with Robert Marzano's new taxonomy of educational objectives. Before we delve into these strategies, however, let's take a closer look at the student population for whom they are designed—the students who are all too often left behind, even in environments that purport to be inclusive.

WHO BENEFITS FROM USE OF THESE STRATEGIES?

As discussed in Chapter 1, this population includes many students with IDs or multiple disabilities such as Down syndrome, autism spectrum disorder, fetal alcohol syndrome, Prader-Willi syndrome, and fragile X syndrome. Although each student is unique, certain characteristics and challenges are common among the student populations for whom these strategies have been designed; these are highlighted in the vignettes below and discussed further in the sections that follow. You may find that you recognize characteristics of your own current or former students. As you read each of the vignettes below, ask yourself:

- What specific skills are especially challenging for this student?

- What supports does this student typically need from teachers and peers?

- How can a teacher play to this student's specific strengths to help the student reach his or her full potential?

Student 1: Ángel, age 17

Ángel, age 17, is a senior attending an inclusive high school. Ángel lives with his parents, Marisol and Miguel, and his 13-year-old sister Caridad. Ángel currently volunteers twice a week at a local nursing home; after graduation, he wants to continue working in geriatric health care in some capacity. He has talked with his IEP team about possibilities such as applying for a full-time position in food preparation or custodial services at the nursing home.

Ángel has a mild ID; he has been diagnosed with Down syndrome. He can read and write at about a fourth-grade level, and he performs at a similar level in math. His favorite subject is science, and he is particularly interested in topics related to anatomy and health, although he struggles with science content that involves math. Ángel is also quite athletic and a member of his high school swim team. His best friend, Roger, is on the team with him, and they spend lots of time together, exercising, watching TV, or just hanging out. Ángel is well liked by other peers and is close to his sister and parents.

Ángel likes how his weekly routine of school, swim practice, household chores, volunteer work, and spending time with friends keeps him busy. He uses a wall calendar to stay organized. At school and at his volunteer job, he is good at remembering and following directions once a procedure has been demonstrated and explained step by step. He gets flustered if he is asked to remember and execute too many steps at once or if something interferes with his daily routine.

Student 2: Tomas, age 12

Tomas is a quiet seventh grader who is passionate about trains. He loves to look at pictures of trains and watch videos of trains, and he knows endless facts about trains. Tomas keeps a scrapbook of pictures and artifacts he finds related to trains. He likes to bring his scrapbook to school and look at it when he is finished his classwork. Sometimes, when prompted by his paraprofessional, he will show his classmates some of his favorite pictures. Tomas is very motivated to learn if the lesson involves trains in some way.

Tomas lives with his mother, and he is an only child. His mother is involved in Tomas' education and attends school meetings and parent–teacher conferences when she is not working. She tries to stay in regular communication with the school because Tomas has an IEP. He was diagnosed with autism spectrum disorder as a young child. He does not speak and instead communicates with gestures, visual aids, and a tablet.

Tomas has cognitive deficits that also impair his ability to learn content at the same level as his classmates. It is challenging for him to think through complex ideas and abstract thoughts. He responds well to activities that are concrete and hands-on. For tasks that involve more than one step, such as adding two-digit numbers with regrouping, his teacher gives him a checklist of steps to follow. He has a collection of these prompt cards for math, which he uses as necessary. Tomas can recognize basic sight words and is learning to spell them. Occasionally, while in class, Tomas will become agitated. His paraprofessional has several social stories on hand to help Tomas self-regulate and calm down. If necessary, he can go to a quiet room in another area of the school where he can put on headphones and listen to calming music.

Even though Tomas does not initiate social interaction, he is learning to respond to people using augmentative communication through his tablet. He requires ongoing support from his teacher and paraprofessional to master independence in this area. Because Tomas has been fully included in school since kindergarten, he is familiar with his classmates. They include Tomas in activities and like to ask him about his favorite subject—trains.

Student 3: Morgan, age 8

Morgan is an 8-year-old girl who attends the local elementary school with her older brother. Morgan is fully included in her third-grade general education class. In her classroom, Morgan enjoys helping the teacher pass out papers and looking at books with her classmates. Her teacher recently brought some jigsaw puzzles to school, which Morgan loves to work on in her free time. Although she is engaged and motivated to learn in the morning, Morgan can get quite tired by the afternoon. In addition, Morgan has a fascination with food. To help Morgan stay focused on learning, her teacher has asked students not to bring any food into the classroom. All food is secured in the cafeteria.

Morgan was diagnosed with Prader-Willi syndrome as a baby. She is gradually meeting most physical milestones and has moderate IDs. Morgan has a good long-term memory but struggles to remember new information. Her teacher often reteaches new concepts with lots of visuals to give Morgan a great deal of time to process the new concepts. Morgan is interested in reading and is learning to recognize basic sight words. She does not like to write, finding it both a physically and a mentally draining task. Morgan finds math very challenging, particularly with problems that take several steps to solve. She finds it hard to process information in small pieces. Morgan works below grade level in both language arts and math, and, as a result, she is on a modified education program for both subjects.

Morgan can become very focused on completing an activity, and she can be very good at finding the information she is looking for. However, she can find it challenging to transition to new tasks. As a result, Morgan can become quite frustrated and upset. Her teacher tries to give her as much warning as possible before a transition takes place. Morgan's teacher and paraprofessional keep the classroom routine as predictable as possible. In addition, they use a daily communication book to keep her parents updated on Morgan's progress and issues.

Summary: Typical Challenges

The challenges faced by Ángel, Tomas, and Morgan are fairly common among students diagnosed with IDs. Each of the students described in the vignettes has strengths, and each also experiences some limitations related to his or her disability. The American Association on Intellectual and Developmental Disabilities (AAIDD) classifies typical limitations in two broad categories, *intellectual functioning* and *adaptive behavior* (AAIDD, 2017). Intellectual functioning encompasses a student's ability to learn new information, solve problems, and reason (AAIDD, 2017). As defined by the AAIDD, adaptive behavior covers three types of skills:

- Conceptual skills—language and literacy; money, time, and number concepts; and self-direction
- Social skills—interpersonal skills, social responsibility, self-esteem, gullibility, naiveté (i.e., wariness)
- Practical skills—activities of daily living (personal care), occupational skills, healthcare, travel/transportation, schedules/routines, safety, use of money, use of the telephone. (AAIDD, 2017)

The precise nature and degree of these limitations vary a great deal among individual students, ranging from mild to moderate or severe. A particular student's challenges are just one factor to consider when planning instruction—it is also vital for teachers to consider that student's strengths. That said, the limitations described previously are linked with particular challenges students with IDs may experience in the classroom that necessitate substantial modifications to the grade-level curriculum. These challenges can include any of the following:

- **Limited working memory abilities,** such as recognizing, recalling, and using information. Students may have difficulty spelling words, recalling math facts, determining true or false information, or naming the letters of the alphabet.

- **Difficulty with comprehension skills** that include summarizing, symbolizing, and explaining. For example, students can find it hard to describe key elements of a story or illustrate what happened in the story.

- **Trouble analyzing information** through processes such as sorting, distinguishing, organizing, assessing, predicting, and generalizing. For example, students with IDs may not be able to apply their knowledge of addition and subtraction to the task of solving a long-division equation.

- **Difficulty with applying their knowledge to complete complex tasks or understand abstract concepts.** Solving problems, experimenting, investigating, and making suitable decisions may be challenging for students with IDs.

HOW TO USE THIS CHAPTER

The 40 strategies described on the following pages are organized according to the framework provided by Marzano's new taxonomy of educational objectives, discussed in Chapter 6. As you read through the strategies, note that they call upon different types of thinking skills. Thus, those presented first involve strategies for developing knowledge retrieval, followed by comprehension, analysis, and knowledge utilization strategies. Remember that, as with the thinking skills in Marzano's taxonomy, the strategies can be learned independently of one another. A student does not need to master the first strategy before moving on to the next. Strategies are chosen for students because they may be the most appropriate choice based on an individual's abilities, needs, and educational goals, and the nature of the content to be learned.

Each strategy includes the following components:

- A **brief description** of the strategy

- **Student goals** related to typical IEP goals used with the student populations discussed in this book

- **Step-by-step directions** for using the strategy. The directions include **suggested interventions** to simplify the strategy based on the student's needs (e.g., using pictures rather than text if a student does not read), **suggested extensions** to increase the challenge as appropriate for the student's ability level (e.g., by elaborating responses in greater detail), and additional **implementation tips.**

- **Student work sample(s)** illustrating how the strategy can be used to modify a grade-level assignment for a student with significant intellectual challenges

- A paragraph providing additional **context** about how the student's modified assignment/activity relates to the grade-level curriculum and/or the student's IEP goals

- Details about what **type of curriculum modification** this strategy represents: changes to content, conceptual difficulty, educational goals, instructional method, or a combination of these

Bear in mind that these curriculum strategies are designed to be usable at any level with different types of content. For each strategy, a student work sample and contextual description are included to give readers a sense of what the strategy looks like in action. However, in each case, the example provided is just one way the strategy can be adapted for a particular curriculum, learning objective, and student. As you read, you will surely have your own ideas about how to apply these strategies with your students to address different curricula and learning objectives and work with individual students' IEP goals.

I. Is It Yes or No?

Students recall information about the lesson concepts. Students affirm or deny statements about the main ideas and/or details of the lesson by indicating *yes* or *no*.

Student Goals

- Determine the correct answer.
- Use recognition skills.
- Develop the ability to follow directions.

Directions for Teachers

1. Identify key facts in the lesson.
2. Using the facts, create very direct questions from the text (or other verbally presented facts) that will elicit *yes* or *no* responses from the student. For example, ask, "Is the dog black?" or "Is an ocean bigger than a stream?"
3. Have the student respond to each question by circling the correct answer.

Interventions

Pictures or symbols can be substituted for written questions and answers.

Questions can be read out loud by a peer, paraprofessional, or teacher.

Responses can be given verbally, using an assistive device, or with a predetermined action such as raising a hand up for *yes* and down for *no*.

The teacher can limit the number of questions asked.

Extensions

The student can finish the response (either orally or in written form) with a complete sentence; for example, "Yes, the dog is black."

The student can create his or her own set of yes/no questions about the content.

The teacher can survey the class and create a class tally of responses.

The student can work with a buddy to answer questions.

The teacher can create a class activity using yes/no questions.

Remember

Ask closed questions to which students can give a definitive answer; for example, "Is this an apple?"

Ensure that each student understands how to give the response.

Allow time for the student to respond.

Context for Student Work Sample

The work sample shown in Figure 7.1 represents an assignment that could be completed by a third-grade student working well below grade level. As part of the math curriculum, this student's classmates are learning to distinguish among different kinds of quadrilaterals, such as rhombuses, rectangles, and squares. For this student, the curriculum content, conceptual difficulty, and educational goals have been modified to focus on distinguishing among basic geometric shapes.

Example: Is It Yes or No?

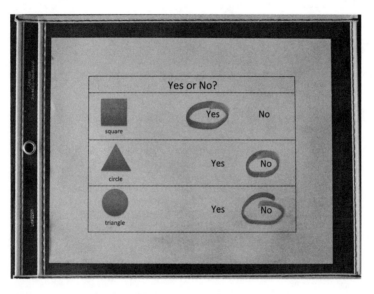

Figure 7.1. A completed, modified activity using the Is It Yes or No? strategy. The student has used a dry-erase pocket to do the activity.

2. Find It

Students reinforce their knowledge by searching for text, numbers, or illustrations in a grade-level activity.

Student Goals

- Find information.
- Select correct information.
- Develop the ability to follow directions.

Directions for Teachers

1. Ask the student to identify specific numbers, letters, or text within the assignment that are related to the student's IEP goals.

2. Have the student circle, highlight, cross out, or point to the answer.

Interventions

Offer hints or prompts, such as, "You will find the answer in the first row."

Reduce the amount of text or numbers, or the number of pictures.

Have the student work with a peer to find the answer.

Extensions

Have the student use the answers in a follow-up activity. For example, if the student was to find words that begin with the letter *a,* have the student make the letter *a* using playdough.

Have the student create his or her own search criteria.

Remember

Ensure that the activity is visually accessible.

Give the student an appropriate tool to find the answer, such as a pencil, a highlighter, or the use of assistive technology.

Context for Student Work Sample

The activity and work sample shown in Figures 7.2 and 7.3 represent how a fifth-grade spelling assignment could be modified for a student working well below grade level. Peers working with the grade-level curriculum are learning to decode and spell multisyllabic words ending in -*ant* and -*able*. For this fifth-grade student, whose IEP goals address letter recognition and learning letter–sound correspondences, the conceptual difficulty and educational goals have been modified to focus on identification of the letter *a*. This student can use the same worksheet peers use, but the oral directions given to the student reflect the different learning goals.

Example: Find It

Name: _____   Date: _____

Grade 5 Spelling Practice

Copy the following words.

servant	
important	
excitable	
pleasant	
participant	
portable	
honorable	
adaptable	
approachable	

Figure 7.2. An example of a typical grade-level activity with which the Find It strategy could be used.

Name: _____   Date: _____

Grade 5 Spelling Practice

~~Copy the following words.~~

servant	
important	
excitable	
pleasant	
participant	
portable	
honorable	
adaptable	
approachable	

Figure 7.3. A completed, modified activity using the Find It strategy. The student was asked to find and mark the letter *a* in the class spelling list.

3. Cross It Out

Grade-level concepts and/or ideas that are not relevant to the student's IEP goals are crossed out. The student learns from the remaining material.

Student Goals

- Recognize a specific item, such as a letter and/or number.
- Demonstrate knowledge.
- Develop the ability to focus.

Directions for Teachers

1. Identify text, numbers, or skills relevant to the student's IEP goals in the class activity.
2. Isolate irrelevant text or numbers on the page by crossing them out with a pen or marker.
3. Have the student complete the portion of the activity that is not crossed out.

Interventions

Enlarge the assignment.

Circle, highlight, or point to the assigned work.

Cover up irrelevant activities with another piece of paper.

Recreate the activity on another piece of paper or on the computer.

Extensions

Guide the student to cross out the text or numbers that he or she will not need to work with.

Have the student determine what material is irrelevant to the task he or she needs to do.

Remember

Keep the student copy as close to the original as possible; modify concepts only as necessary.

Monitor the student's ability to focus only on his or her assigned work.

Context for Student Work Sample

The activity and work sample shown in Figures 7.4 and 7.5 illustrate how a third-grade mathematics assignment could be modified for a student working well below grade level. Peers working with the grade-level curriculum are learning to subtract three-digit numbers. For this student, the conceptual difficulty, educational goals, and instructional method have been modified to focus on subtraction of single-digit numbers. Again, the student uses the same worksheet peers use, but it is modified to fit the student's different skill level.

Example: Cross It Out

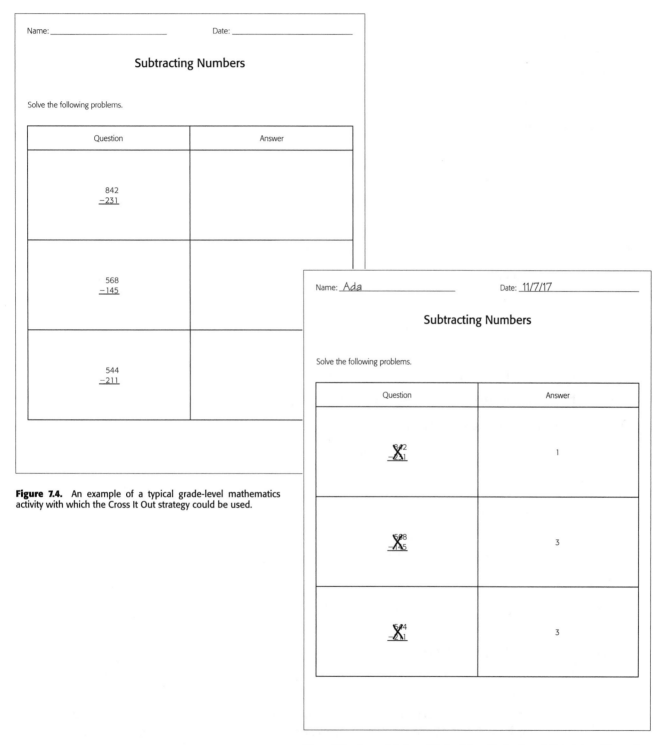

Figure 7.4. An example of a typical grade-level mathematics activity with which the Cross It Out strategy could be used.

Figure 7.5. A completed, modified activity using the Cross It Out strategy. The student was asked to solve the simpler math problems the teacher created by using the strategy.

4. Substitute It

Students can use a grade-level activity to work with ability-level concepts by working on an alternate goal.

Student Goals

- Execute developmentally appropriate skills.
- Demonstrate knowledge.
- Work with grade-level content.

Directions for Teachers

1. Prior to the class activity, determine what concepts can be altered, deleted, or changed to align with the student's IEP goals.
2. Use as much of the original activity as possible to create the modified work.
3. Have the student complete the activity.

Interventions

Rewrite the modifications in an alternate format to reduce confusion with the existing lesson.

Cover up material that is not relevant to the task the student is being asked to do.

Have the student work with learning materials to complete the answer.

Reduce the amount of work to be done.

Ensure that there is enough space on the activity worksheet for the student to work in.

Extensions

Ask the student to create the modified questions.

Have the student recreate the modified activity in another format. For example, the student can print it, use manipulatives, use a computer, or present it to the class.

Remember

The student may also be interested in the grade-level activity, so be willing to provide further instruction or explanation.

Context for Student Work Sample

The activity and work sample shown in Figures 7.6 and 7.7 illustrate how a fifth-grade mathematics assignment could be modified for a student working well below grade level. Peers working with the grade-level curriculum are learning to work with percentages and decimals, including using knowledge thereof to solve word problems that require them to complete several steps. For this student, the curriculum content, conceptual difficulty, and educational goals have been modified to focus on addition of two-digit numbers. The instructional method has been modified to have the student complete a math goal that does not include the more complex reasoning involved in solving a word problem (reading the problem, determining which math tasks need to be completed and in what order, and then completing them).

Example: Substitute It

Name: _____ Date: _____

Word Problems With Decimals

Solve the following problems.

Question	Answer
Josh mows lawns. He gets $45 a day. He works 22.5 days in a month. How much money will he earn in a month?	
Kristen went to a clothing store. She bought a pair of jeans for $23.55, a sweater for $30.01 and a shirt for $16. Now she has $20 left. How much money did she have to start with?	
Peter purchased a toy car for $6.75 and spent $12.50 on a book. If he started with $25, how much does he have left?	

Figure 7.6. An example of a typical grade-level mathematics activity with which the Substitute It strategy could be used.

Name: _Marcus_____ Date: _10/3/17_____

Word Problems With Decimals

Solve the following problems.

Question	Answer
Josh mows lawns. He gets $45 a day. He works 22.5 days in a month. How much money will he earn in a month 45 +22	45 +22 67
Kristen went to a clothing store. She bought a pair of jeans for $23.55, a sweater for $30.01 and a shirt for $16. Now she has $20 left. How much money did she have to start with? 23 +16	23 +16 39
Peter purchased a toy car for $6.75 and spent $12.50 on a book. If he started with $25, how much money does he have left? 12 +25	12 +25 37

Figure 7.7. A completed, modified activity using the Substitute It strategy. The teacher used the same numbers used in the word problems but had the student add them.

5. Identify It

Students identify a developmentally appropriate concept within an existing activity or assignment.

Student Goals

- Identify accurate information.
- Locate information.

Directions for Teachers

1. Print a copy of the Identify It organizer. (See Form 2 in Appendix B for a printable template.)
2. Review the concepts that the student is to identify.
3. Have the student identify the concepts and record them in the graphic organizer.

Interventions

Limit the number of concepts for the student to identify.

Scribe the student's responses.

Have the student use pictures or symbols to represent answers.

Extensions

Have the student identify increasingly difficult concepts.

Ask the student to determine the concepts that he or she will identify.

Have the student identify the concepts and use them in an alternate activity. For example, if the student is asked to identify vocabulary, then have the student use the vocabulary words in sentences.

Remember

The student can work independently or with a group to identify the concepts.

Context for Student Work Sample

The work sample shown in Figure 7.8 shows how a fifth-grade English language arts assignment could be modified for a student working below grade level. The class is learning how to determine the meaning of words and phrases as they are used in text, distinguishing fact from opinion; they have been asked to apply this skill to a nonfiction passage about the history of television (not shown here). Using the same grade-level passage of nonfiction text about the history of television as the class, the conceptual difficulty, educational goals, and instructional method of the assignment were modified for the student. The student worked with a paraprofessional to identify three facts about the history of television and record them on the graphic organizer.

Example: Identify It

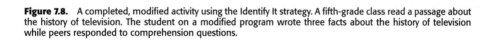

Name: _Josh_____   Date: _2/27/18_____

Identify It

1. John Baird made the first television.

2. The first TV was made in 1925.

3. The first color TV was made in 1953.

Figure 7.8.   A completed, modified activity using the Identify It strategy. A fifth-grade class read a passage about the history of television. The student on a modified program wrote three facts about the history of television while peers responded to comprehension questions.

6. Who, When, and Where Is It?

Students gather information from a text to convey details in the story, such as who is in the story, when the story happened, and where it took place.

Student Goals

- Recall key events.
- Describe key events.
- Develop the ability to summarize information.

Directions for Teachers

1. Print a copy of the Who, When, and Where Is It? graphic organizer. (See Form 3 in Appendix B for a printable template.)
2. Have the student use the organizer to recall the details of the story.
3. Encourage the student to refer back to the text to locate answers.

Interventions

Identify the details in the text before transcribing them into the graphic organizer. Underline or highlight them for the student.

Limit the number of details.

Use pictures or symbols to represent details instead of words.

Extensions

Add more complexity to the assignment, such as having the student answer *how* and *why* questions about the story.

Illustrate the details.

Have the student write answers in complete sentences.

Remember

Students can benefit from working in groups for this strategy.

Encourage the student to give as much detail about the text as possible.

Context for Student Work Sample

The work sample shown in Figure 7.9 illustrates how a student with reading skills below grade level could work with a literary text typically assigned in Grade 8 or 9. Peers working within the grade-level curriculum are reading Harper Lee's *To Kill a Mockingbird* and are learning to cite explicitly the textual evidence that most strongly supports an analysis of what the text says. In this example, the assignment has been modified for the student. She has been asked to answer questions that demonstrate her understanding of the text, referring explicitly to the text as the basis for the answers. This represents a modification of conceptual difficulty, educational goals, and instructional method, but the student is nevertheless learning to use textual evidence as the basis for her responses as her peers are also learning to do.

Example: Who, When, and Where Is It?

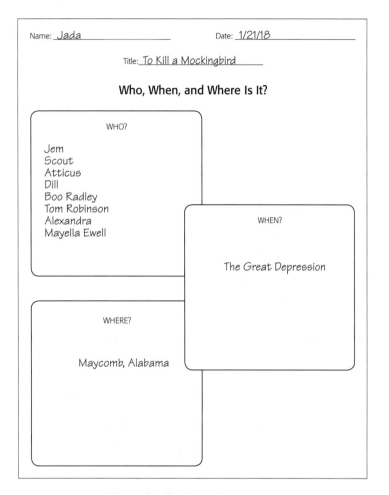

Name: _Jada_____   Date: _1/21/18_____

Title: _To Kill a Mockingbird_____

Who, When, and Where Is It?

WHO?

Jem
Scout
Atticus
Dill
Boo Radley
Tom Robinson
Alexandra
Mayella Ewell

WHEN?

The Great Depression

WHERE?

Maycomb, Alabama

Figure 7.9. A completed, modified activity using the Who, When, and Where Is It? strategy. An eighth-grade class used textual evidence to support their analysis of the novel *To Kill a Mockingbird;* this student used textual evidence to record details about the characters, setting, and plot.

7. Label It

Students learn new vocabulary associated with the lesson.

Student Goals

- Recognize new vocabulary.

- Demonstrate understanding of new vocabulary.

- Expand personal use of vocabulary.

Directions for Teachers

1. Identify the vocabulary in the activity that will support the student's IEP goals.

2. Using the class activity, introduce new vocabulary related to the lesson. Discuss the meaning and usage of the new words.

3. Write the vocabulary words on index cards, on paper, or on the computer. Have students practice recognizing and using the vocabulary words. (In this example, the student uses words from his cards to label a diagram.)

4. Collect the cards and keep the vocabulary words on hand to create a personal word bank for the student.

Interventions

Use computer-generated pictures and/or symbols to represent the vocabulary word(s).

Have students create a representation of the vocabulary word(s), such as a model or models.

Limit the number of vocabulary words for the student to learn.

Scribe the word(s) for the student.

Extensions

Have the student choose vocabulary words with which to work.

Include the definition of each word.

Have the student independently type or write the vocabulary card.

Create a set of cards with vocabulary words. Create a second set with definitions of the vocabulary words. Have students match up vocabulary words with definitions.

Encourage the student to use new vocabulary words in speech or written work.

Remember

Presume competence and provide students with words that can challenge them and extend their thinking skills.

Context for Student Work Sample

The student activity and work sample shown in Figures 7.10 and 7.11 illustrate how a fifth-grade student working below grade level could learn vocabulary related to the grade-level curriculum and to the student's IEP goals. Peers working within the grade-level curriculum are learning about the human body and working with the vocabulary words and skeleton diagram shown in Figure 7.10. Relatedly, this student's IEP team has set a goal that the student will learn at least five new vocabulary words related to this curriculum unit. After learning, using word cards (not shown) to learn his assigned list of words, the student uses the words to complete the modified labeling activity shown in Figure 7.11. This assignment involves modifications to conceptual difficulty and educational goals, but the student is nevertheless working with content and skills related to the grade-level curriculum.

Example: Label It

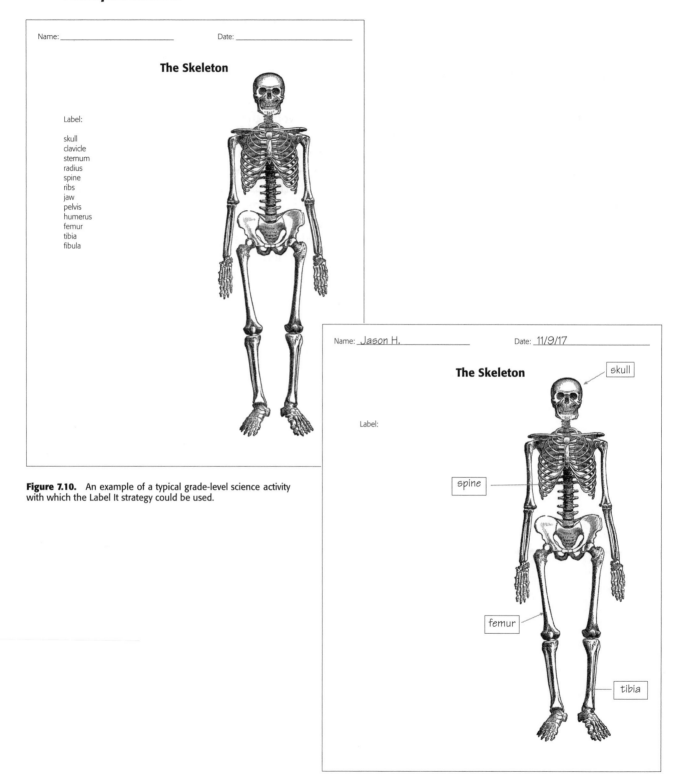

Figure 7.10.   An example of a typical grade-level science activity with which the Label It strategy could be used.

Figure 7.11.   A completed, modified activity using the Label It strategy. The student uses this activity to work on learning vocabulary words related to his individualized education program goals.

8. Highlight It

Students learn relevant vocabulary, numbers, and concepts that are highlighted within the lesson or activity.

Student Goals

- Identify correct information.
- Develop the ability to locate information.
- Select the appropriate answer.

Directions for Teachers

1. Using a copy of the class activity, provide the student with a list of vocabulary words, numbers, or concepts that are important to the lesson and aligned with the student's IEP goals.
2. Review the list to ensure that the student understands what he or she is looking for.
3. Have the student find and highlight the listed vocabulary words, numbers, or text in the class assignment. Provide support, if needed.
4. Have the student work with the highlighted material to complete either the class assignment or a related activity.

Interventions

Highlight for the student.

Isolate and rewrite the highlighted text.

Use pictures in association with highlighted text to facilitate comprehension.

Enlarge the text for accessibility.

Extensions

Assign different colors of highlighter for different types of vocabulary or text. For example, a blue highlighter can be used for words and a yellow highlighter for numbers.

Use the highlighted text or numbers in a follow-up activity. For example, the student can highlight spelling words and put them in sentences.

Remember

The student can work with a buddy to complete the assignment.

Ensure that the student can use the highlighting tool.

Context for Student Work Samples

The activity and work sample shown in Figures 7.12 and 7.13 demonstrate how a student who reads below grade level can meet an IEP-related standard that is within the same English language arts strand that his typically developing peers are working on. In this assignment, fourth-grade students are learning how to answer questions about the topic by referring back to the text, as shown in Figure 7.12. Figure 7.13 shows how the assignment has been modified to help the student answer questions about the text, using highlighted text to prompt and guide the student's response. This represents a modification of conceptual difficulty, educational goals, and instructional method.

Example: Highlight It

Name: _____   Date: _____

Species

Read the passage below.
Answer the questions.

A group of animals that look alike are named a species. An example of a species would be snakes. Snakes are a very important part of the world around us. They eat a variety of prey including mice, birds, and frogs. Snakes have hinged jaws, which means they can open their mouth very wide. They can eat food that is wider than their own bodies! Snakes also have forked tongues. Their tongue helps them find their way around in the dark. Snakes like to be left alone. Some are dangerous and harmful to humans. Keep your distance from snakes and let them do their job for our environment!

1. What is a group of animals that look alike called?
   _____

2. What do snakes like to eat?
   _____

3. Why do snakes have forked tongues?

   _____

Figure 7.12. An example of a typical grade-level reading comprehension activity with which the Highlight It strategy could be used.

Name: _Robert_____   Date: _9/12/17_____

Species

Read the passage below.
Answer the questions.

A group of animals that look alike are named a species. An example of a species would be snakes. Snakes are a very important part of the world around us. They eat a variety of prey including mice, birds, and frogs. Snakes have hinged jaws, which means they can open their mouth very wide. They can eat food that is wider than their own bodies! Snakes also have forked tongues. Their tongue helps them find their way around in the dark. Snakes like to be left alone. Some are dangerous and harmful to humans. Keep your distance from snakes and let them do their job for our environment!

1. What is a group of animals that look alike called?
   _species_____

2. What do snakes like to eat?
   _mice, birds, and frogs_____

3. Why do snakes have forked tongues?
   Their tongue helps them find their way around
   _in the dark._____

Figure 7.13. A completed, modified activity using the Highlight It strategy. The passage the student reads is the same as the one his peers read, but highlighting makes key details easier to find.

9. Spell It

Students find developmentally appropriate spelling words embedded in grade-level spelling words.

Student Goals

- Recognize vocabulary words.

- Demonstrate spelling skills.

- Locate information.

Directions for Teachers

1. Within the class spelling list, identify goal-appropriate text embedded within the words, such as letters, letter blends, or smaller words.

2. Highlight the relevant text within the spelling word(s).

3. Have the student learn to spell, pronounce, or recognize the embedded text.

Interventions

Use a cloze technique to help the student print the ability-level word.

Recreate a list of ability-level words only.

Allow the student to trace over or type out words rather than writing them.

Have the student practice spelling words through various activities, such as matching the same word, spelling it out in sand, or using different colors to print the word.

Extensions

Have the student independently find the word and rewrite it for practice.

Have the student learn to spell larger portions of the word.

Have the student participate in the class spelling practice and/or test using his or her word list.

Have the student practice spelling the words through activities such as crosswords, word searches, and spelling games.

Remember

The student can type the words, have a buddy scribe, or use speech-to-text software for greater accessibility.

Context for Student Work Samples

The activity and work sample shown in Figures 7.14 and 7.15 illustrate how a fifth-grade student who works below grade level in reading and spelling can learn to spell developmentally appropriate words embedded in the more complex list of words with which his peers are working. Using the class spelling list, the teacher has identified single-syllable words with common spelling patterns embedded within the larger words. The student has been asked to learn how to spell his modified words. This example represents a modification of conceptual difficulty, educational goals, and instructional method.

STRATEGIES FOR KNOWLEDGE RETRIEVAL

● ●

Example: Spell It

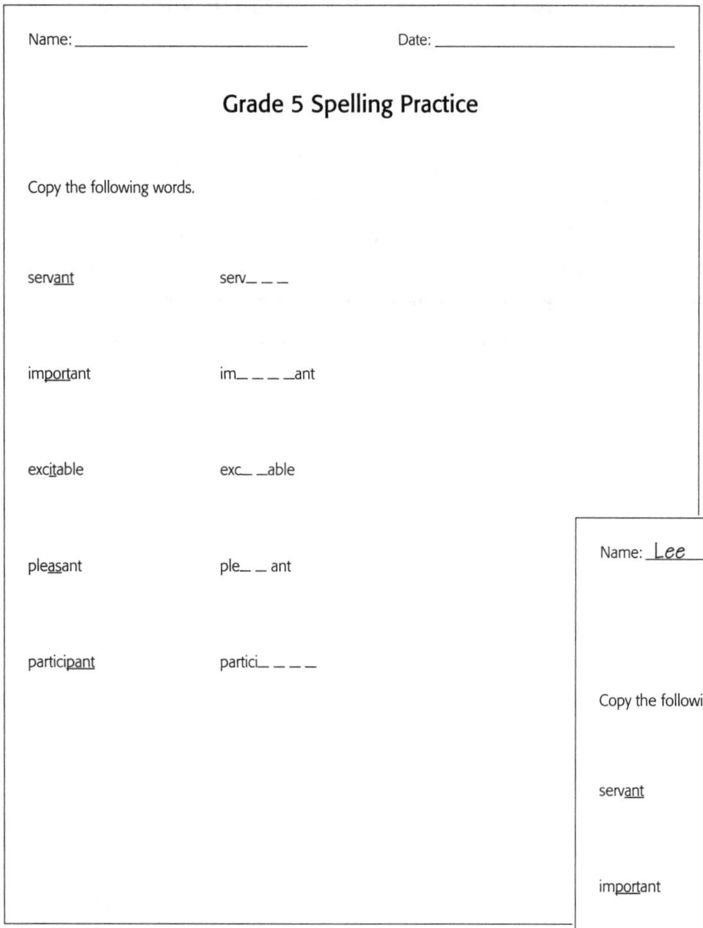

Name: _____   Date: _____

Grade 5 Spelling Practice

Copy the following words.

serv<u>ant</u>   serv_ _ _

im<u>por</u>tant   im_ _ _ _ant

exc<u>it</u>able   exc_ _able

ple<u>as</u>ant   ple_ _ ant

partici<u>pant</u>   partici_ _ _ _

Figure 7.14. An example of how a teacher would use the Spell It strategy to modify a worksheet with a typical grade-level spelling activity.

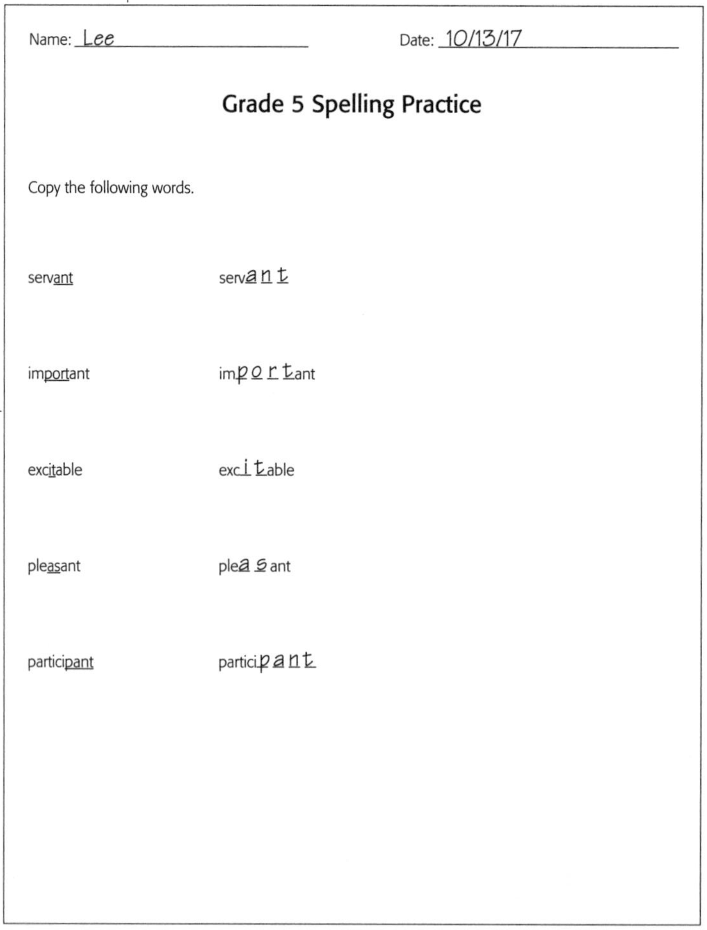

Name: <u>Lee</u>   Date: <u>10/13/17</u>

Grade 5 Spelling Practice

Copy the following words.

serv<u>ant</u>   serva n t

im<u>por</u>tant   imp o r tant

exc<u>it</u>able   exc i table

ple<u>as</u>ant   ple a s ant

partici<u>pant</u>   partici p a n t

Figure 7.15. An example of student work on the assignment created using the Spell It strategy.

10. It's a Letter Clue

Students complete an activity or assignment using letter clues.

Student Goals

- Develop recall ability.
- Demonstrate knowledge of vocabulary.
- Predict information based on clues.

Directions for Teachers

1. Using the class activity or a related activity, provide letters and/or a combination of letters that will provide a clue to the answer. For example, if the correct answer is a phrase, the first letter of each word can be given to prompt a response.

2. Encourage the student to check if the answer makes sense.

Interventions

Begin by giving as many clues as possible and then gradually scale back the support.

Provide a word bank for the student to use while printing the answer.

Print the answers and have the student trace over them.

Extensions

Give the student a phrase or sentence to complete using the prompts.

Leave out the letter prompt if the student can independently answer the question.

Switch the placement of the letter prompt from the beginning of the word to the middle or the end.

Use this activity within the text a student is working with. Cover up a word with a sticky note, leaving the first letter visible.

Have the student verbally predict and/or write the word.

Remember

Recreate the activity on an assistive device, use it with a dry-erase pocket, or enlarge it for greater accessibility.

Ensure the student has enough space for his or her response.

Context for Student Work Sample

The work sample shown in Figure 7.16 shows how a fourth-grade student reading below grade level could learn vocabulary related to the grade-level curriculum. Peers working within the grade-level curriculum are learning vocabulary words related to the water cycle. Meanwhile, the student's IEP team has set a goal that the student will learn how to spell five words related to this curriculum unit. In this example, the student is learning to spell the word *blue* because the color blue is typically used to represent water on diagrams of the water cycle. Using the gradual reduction of letter clues, the student learns how to spell the new word in this assignment. The example shows a modification in content, concept, educational goals, and instructional method.

Example: It's a Letter Clue

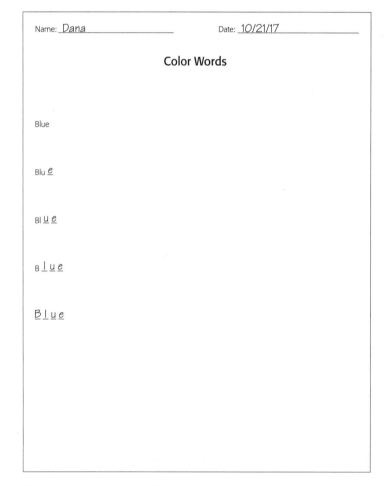

Figure 7.16. A completed, modified activity using the It's a Letter Clue strategy.

II. Use It in a Sentence

Students are asked to demonstrate their understanding of a concept by using words related to it in a sentence.

Student Goals

- Demonstrate understanding of new concepts.

- Demonstrate use of the new concept.

- Improve reading and/or writing skills.

Directions for Teachers

1. Teach and review the new concept.

2. Ask the student to use words related to the new concept in a sentence. Provide a sentence frame to help the student do this. For example, if the student is learning about the relationship between exercise and health, have the student complete the sentence frame, *An exercise I like is _____.*

3. Have the student (or scribe) write out the sentence on a sentence strip (or use another developmentally appropriate medium for written work, such as an iPad).

Interventions

Use visuals to further support the student's understanding of the sentence he or she needs to complete by using the new words and concept.

Simplify the type of sentence to be created.

Have the student work with a buddy to reread the sentence(s) he or she has created.

Extensions

Increase the complexity of the sentences to be completed.

Teach the student different types of sentences, such as statements and questions, or simple, compound, and complex sentences.

Have the student reread the sentences he or she has created to a buddy or into an audio recording device.

Have the student create the sentences independently, without using a teacher-created sentence frame.

Remember

Increase student engagement by creating interesting sentences.

Keep the sentence strips as a reference or form of practice.

Students can work with the vocabulary words in the sentences. For example, students can create a visual for each word or use the words in a vocabulary game.

Context for Student Work Sample

The work sample shown in Figure 7.17 shows how a fifth-grade student working below grade level can learn health education with his same-grade peers. The class has been learning to use a decision-making process to determine personal choices that promote personal, environmental, and community health. They have been asked to keep a daily log of their healthy habits for 1 week. Meanwhile, the student is asked to describe ways in which he participates regularly in active play and enjoyable physical activities. He has chosen to write four sentences about playing with a ball. The assignment has been modified in conceptual difficulty, educational goals, and instructional method.

Example: Use It in a Sentence

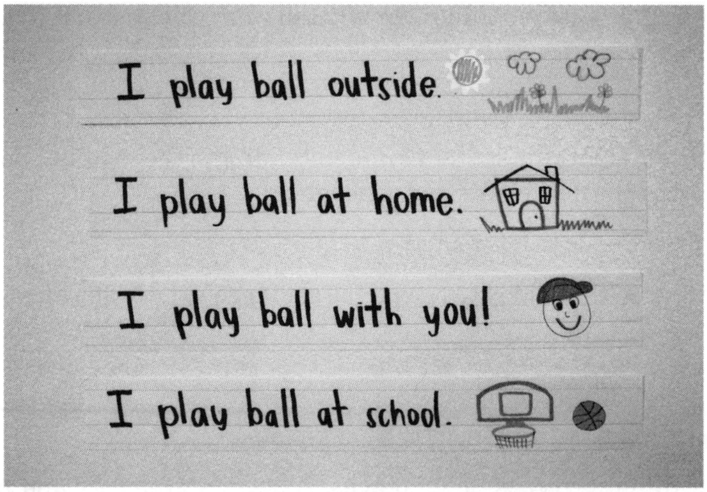

Figure 7.17. Sentence strips used with the Use It in a Sentence strategy. (Photo by Kristen Eredics.)

12. It's a Number Clue

Students solve a mathematical problem using number clues.

Student Goals

- Use recognition skills.
- Recall accurate information.
- Develop ability to predict.

Directions for Teachers

1. Create developmentally appropriate number clues in the class activity to prompt student response. The clues can be used for eliciting an answer or explaining a process. As a simple example, if the student is still learning to recognize numbers in word form, the word *eight* can be changed to the number 8. Another example would be simplifying long, multistep equations.

2. Have the student complete the assignment or related activity.

Interventions

Scribe the entire answer for the student.

Print the answers and have the student trace over them.

Provide a number chart for the student to refer to.

Extensions

Reduce the total of number clues provided.

Eliminate the number clue.

Remember

If needed, provide the student with a calculator for computation questions.

This strategy can be used on paper, on the computer, or with manipulatives.

Context for Student Work Sample

The activity and work sample shown in Figures 7.18 and 7.19 show how a fourth-grade student working below grade level in mathematics can learn with fourth-grade math material. Peers have been learning to interpret multiplication problems, as shown in the class worksheet in Figure 7.18. Meanwhile, the student is learning his 2 and 3 times tables. The teacher has modified the class worksheet by simplifying the equations and providing number prompts to help the student solve problems related to this skill, as shown in Figure 7.19. This math assignment has been modified by conceptual difficulty, educational goals, and instructional method. In this way, the student uses a modified version of the same worksheet his peers use, but he practices the mathematics tasks appropriate to his level of skill development.

• •

STRATEGIES FOR KNOWLEDGE RETRIEVAL

Example: It's a Number Clue

Name: _____ Date: _____

Interpreting Multiplication Problems
Grade 4 Math

Complete the sentences.

1. 2 times as many as 2 is ____.

2. 2 times as many as 3 is ____.

3. 42 is ____ times as many as 7.

4. 5 times as many as 3 is ____.

5. 38 is 5 times as many as ____.

Figure 7.18. An example of a typical grade-level mathematics activity with which the It's a Number Clue strategy could be used.

Name: *Elise* _____ Date: 11/10/17 _____

Interpreting Multiplication Problems
Grade 4 Math

~~Complete the sentences.~~

1. 2 times as many as 2 is ____. $2 \times 2 = 4$

2. 2 times as many as 3 is ____. $2 \times 3 = 6$

3. 42 is ____ times as many as 7.

4. 5 times as many as 3 is ____. $5 \times 3 = 15$

5. 38 is 5 times as many as ____.

Figure 7.19. A completed, modified activity using the It's a Number Clue strategy to allow the student to work with multiplication concepts appropriate to his developmental level.

13. List It

Students create lists of concepts, words, or numbers that are relevant to the lesson.

Student Goals

- Use recall skills.
- Develop sorting skills.
- Develop decision-making skills.

Directions for Teachers

1. Print a copy of the List It graphic organizer. (See Form 4 in Appendix B for a printable template.)

2. Determine a topic that is related to the class lesson. Identify two categories within the topic. For example, the topic can be "animals," with a category for small animals and a category for large animals.

3. Have the student sort ideas, words, and/or manipulatives according to the categories within the topic.

4. The student can record answers on the List It graphic organizer.

Interventions

Ask the student to create one list instead of two.

Provide a word bank for the student to use when categorizing.

Give the student pictures to use when categorizing.

Scribe words for the student.

Have the student point to items that can be placed on the list.

Enrichment

Predetermine the length of the list.

Create more complex categories for the topic.

Have the student learn how to spell the list words or use them in an assignment.

Remember

Give the student a choice of topic and categories, when possible.

Give the student a choice in how to represent the list.

This activity can be done with a partner or in groups.

Context for Student Work Sample

The work sample shown in Figure 7.20 demonstrates how a student who works below grade level can meet an IEP-related standard using the same type of instructional method that is used by her peers. The class has been learning about land biomes. Peers have been asked to work on a categorizing activity by using a graphic organizer to list each biome and two or more animals that live in each biome. Meanwhile, the student works on a modified assignment with concepts that are developmentally appropriate and familiar to the student. She uses the graphic organizer to group and list individual sports and team sports. This represents a modification of content, conceptual difficulty, and educational goals.

Example: List It

Name: Lily	Date: 4/5/18

List It

Topic: Sports	
Individual	Team
tennis	hockey
golf	volleyball
swim	basketball
run	water polo
ski	soccer
cycle	baseball

Figure 7.20. A completed, modified activity using the List It strategy to provide the student with practice classifying.

14. Copy It

Students copy words to develop understanding of grade-level concepts.

Student Goals

- Learn how to read new vocabulary.
- Learn how to spell new vocabulary.
- Develop eye–hand coordination.

Directions for Teachers

1. Within a grade-level activity, identify words that will help the student understand lesson concept(s).

2. Have the student copy the assigned word(s) onto the same paper or copy them in another suitable format.

Interventions

Use the hand-over-hand technique to help the student copy the word(s).

Isolate and enlarge the word(s) to be copied.

Give the student tracing paper to use if the student is having difficulty copying.

Extensions

Have the student choose what needs to be copied.

Have the student choose the way in which he or she would like to copy the word(s).

The student can use the copied word(s) in another activity, such as art, music, or language arts.

Remember

Students can also copy lines, shapes, and illustrations depending on the child's ability and the level of complexity in the activity.

Context for Student Work Sample

The work sample shown in Figure 7.21 represents how a second-grade science assignment could be modified for a student working below grade level. Peers working with the grade-level curriculum are learning about plant life cycles. For this student, whose IEP goals address content-related vocabulary, the activity involves reading and copying four vocabulary words related to plants to aid in learning the words' definitions. The assignment has been modified by conceptual difficulty, educational goals, and instructional method.

Example: Copy It

Name: _Sara_____   Date: _2/14/18_____

Copy the following words.

petal	petal
leaf	leaf
stem	stem
roots	roots

Figure 7.21. A completed, modified activity using the Copy It strategy to help the student learn vocabulary related to the grade-level curriculum.

15. Show It

Students demonstrate an understanding of developmentally appropriate concepts by pointing, showing, or outlining what they know.

Student Goals

- Recall new information.
- Develop eye–hand coordination.
- Develop tracking skills.

Directions for Teachers

1. Prepare a grade-level lesson and identify concepts therein that are aligned with the student's IEP goals.
2. Prepare a developmentally appropriate activity that the student can use to show understanding of concepts from the class lesson.
3. Teach the student concepts that are related to the class lesson.
4. Check for understanding through oral prompts asking the student to show what he and/or she has learned from the lesson.

Interventions

Give the student more specific prompts related to the lesson that elicit more specific responses (e.g., present two or three answer choices in the prompt, rather than having the student generate the answer).

Provide a variety of developmentally appropriate materials and methods (e.g., assistive technology, pointers, peer supports, and symbols) to help the student show his or her understanding of concepts.

Extensions

Have the student choose how he or she would like to show understanding of lesson concepts.

Increase the complexity of concepts that the student is expected to understand.

Remember

Reteach the lesson if the student is unable to show what he or she has learned.

Context for Student Work Samples

The activity and work sample shown in Figure 7.22 and Figure 7.23 represent a modified response to a high school quiz on the structures of the eye. High school peers working with the grade-level curriculum are reviewing the anatomy of the eye and will take a unit quiz focused on the structures of the eyeball, as shown in Figure 7.22. Meanwhile, this student has also learned the basic structures of the eyeball. The teacher orally presents questions 2, 3, 4, and 5 and has asked the student to point to show her where the basic structures of the eyeball are located. In response, the student accurately points to the structures on an enlarged illustration, as shown in Figure 7.23. This assignment has been modified by conceptual difficulty, educational goals, and instructional method.

Example: Show It

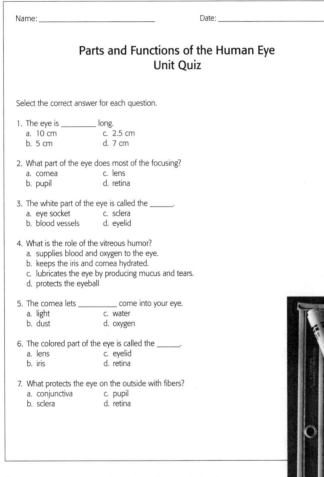

Name: _____   Date: _____

Parts and Functions of the Human Eye
Unit Quiz

Select the correct answer for each question.

1. The eye is _____ long.
   a. 10 cm   c. 2.5 cm
   b. 5 cm   d. 7 cm

2. What part of the eye does most of the focusing?
   a. cornea   c. lens
   b. pupil   d. retina

3. The white part of the eye is called the _____.
   a. eye socket   c. sclera
   b. blood vessels d. eyelid

4. What is the role of the vitreous humor?
   a. supplies blood and oxygen to the eye.
   b. keeps the iris and cornea hydrated.
   c. lubricates the eye by producing mucus and tears.
   d. protects the eyeball

5. The cornea lets _____ come into your eye.
   a. light   c. water
   b. dust   d. oxygen

6. The colored part of the eye is called the _____.
   a. lens   c. eyelid
   b. iris   d. retina

7. What protects the eye on the outside with fibers?
   a. conjunctiva c. pupil
   b. sclera   d. retina

Figure 7.22. An example of a typical grade-level activity with which the Show It strategy could be used.

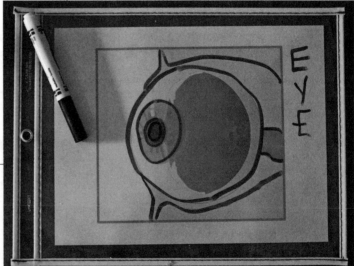

Figure 7.23. A completed, modified activity using the Show It strategy to help the student learn the some of same anatomical concepts covered in the grade-level quiz.

STRATEGIES FOR KNOWLEDGE RETRIEVAL

16. Follow It

Students use a series of written or visual steps as prompts for solving a problem.

Student Goals

- Complete a series of steps to complete an activity.

- Recall information.

- Develop the ability to follow directions.

Directions for Teachers

1. Use with content that requires a series of steps to solve a problem or come to a conclusion.

2. Use either visuals or text to record steps that the student can take to solve the problem. (See Form 5 in Appendix B for a printable template that can be used for addition of two-digit numbers with regrouping; consider creating similar templates for other mathematics content.)

3. Have the student complete the assignment while referring to the instructions.

Interventions

Use visuals instead of words to prompt the student.

Create a bank of problem-solving steps for the student to keep for future reference.

Support the student through each step in the process.

Have a peer model the steps to solving the problem.

Extensions

Gradually reduce the number of steps given to the student.

Have the student create his or her own set of instructions; provide guidance as needed, but let the student take the primary role in identifying the steps and listing them in the correct sequence.

Remember

This strategy can benefit other students who also struggle with multistep instruction.

The strategy can be presented to small groups, large groups, or the whole class.

Students can make a game of giving one another written instructions to complete a task.

Context for Student Work Sample

The work sample shown in Figure 7.24 illustrates how a mathematics equation can be modified for a student who works below grade level and has short-term memory issues. The teacher has taught the class how to solve a mathematical problem with multiple steps—specifically, addition of two-digit numbers that involves regrouping, a task typically learned in Grades 1 and 2. The student's IEP team has recommended that complex assignments be broken down into simple steps. Therefore, the teacher has provided a breakdown of steps for the student to follow in order to solve the equation. This assignment has been modified by conceptual difficulty, educational goals, and instructional method.

Example: Follow It

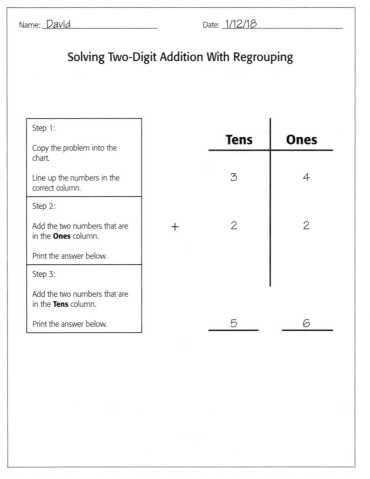

Figure 7.24. A completed, modified activity using the Follow It strategy to help the student follow the steps involved in addition with regrouping.

17. Retell It

Students retell the main events of a story.

Student Goals

- Summarize information.
- Develop sequencing skills.
- Develop understanding of story structure.

Directions for Teachers

1. Print a copy of the Retell It graphic organizer. (See Form 6 in Appendix B for a printable template.)
2. Read and review a story with the student.
3. Discuss events at the beginning, middle, and end of the story. Review the type of information that is important to the reader, such as the characters, setting, and time frame. (This organizer and activity can also be used with any informational text that has a narrative structure, such as biographies or accounts of historical events.)
4. Have the student complete the Retell It graphic organizer. The student can use text or illustrations or give a verbal response.

Interventions

Provide opportunities to discuss and clarify understanding of the story.

Have the student use pictures to represent the story events.

Have the student illustrate one or two parts of the story. For example, have the student retell what occurred in the beginning of the story.

Scribe the student's responses.

Extensions

Have the student provide a more detailed description of the story events. For example, the student can include all of the characters' names, dates, and places.

The student can provide a review of the story and retell his or her favorite part.

Remember

Give the student a choice of reading material when appropriate.

Make it a class event. Have students in the class read separate stories and then have each retell the story they read to a partner.

Context for Student Work Sample

The work sample shown in Figure 7.25 represents a modified English language arts assignment. An eighth-grade class has been asked to complete a detailed summary of *The Hunger Games* by Suzanne Collins. The examples show how the assignment can be modified for a student working well below grade level. For this student, whose IEP goals address retelling the main events in a story, the curriculum content, conceptual difficulty, educational goals, and instructional method have been modified to focus on noting the beginning, middle, and end of the story.

Example: Retell It

Name: _Leah_ _____   Date: _3/15/18_ _____

Retell It

Beginning	Middle	End
Katniss has a sister who is chosen for the Hunger Games. Katniss goes instead.	Katniss and Peta fight together for their lives.	Katniss and Peta win the games.

Figure 7.25. A completed, modified activity using the Retell It strategy to allow the student to summarize major events of a story.

18. Choose It

Students determine the correct answer from a list of choices.

Student Goals

- Distinguish between two answers.
- Locate information.
- Develop decision-making skills.

Directions for Teachers

1. As a follow-up to a class activity, identify comprehension questions that align with the student's IEP goals.

2. List two or three answers for each question. This can be done on the same page or in an alternate format.

3. Have the student choose the correct answer.

Interventions

Pictures or symbols can be substituted for questions and answers.

Questions can be read out loud by a peer, paraprofessional, or teacher.

The student's responses can be given verbally or with a predetermined action.

Limit the number of questions asked.

Extensions

The number of answers can be increased.

The questions can be more complex.

The student can choose an answer and then use it in a sentence.

Remember

Remind the student to refer to the text to find or confirm the answer.

Context for Student Work Sample

The work samples shown in Figures 7.26 and 7.27 show how a third-grade English language arts assignment could be modified for a student working below grade level. Peers working with the grade-level curriculum are learning to read and respond to nonfiction text. They will read a three-paragraph informational text about butterflies and then write the answers to three comprehension questions, as shown in Figure 7.26. All of the questions are literal, not inferential, and the information needed to answer the questions is directly stated in the text. For this student, the teacher has modified the work by providing two answers for the student to choose from, as shown in Figure 7.27. Answering the questions correctly still requires recollection of the facts in the passage, but the cognitive demand on the student is reduced. Thus, the assignment has been modified by conceptual difficulty, educational goals, and instructional method.

Example: Choose It

Name: _____   Date: _____

Butterflies

Butterflies can be found around the world. They come in all sizes, colors, and shapes. There are close to 20,000 types of butterflies. They are interesting to study!

A butterfly has a life cycle that is in four stages. The first stage is the egg stage, followed by the larva stage. The larva is a caterpillar, which eats as much as possible so it can grow into a butterfly. As the caterpillar grows, it loses its exoskeleton. This can happen several times. After a couple of weeks, the caterpillar enters the next stage, which is called the chrysalis. In the chrysalis stage, the caterpillar will become a butterfly.

Answer the following questions:

How many types of butterflies are there?

_____

In what stage does the caterpillar become a butterfly?

_____

How many stages of the butterfly life cycle are there?

_____

Figure 7.26. An example of a typical grade-level activity with which the Choose It strategy could be used.

Name: Ravi   Date: 9/21/17

Butterflies

Butterflies can be found around the world. They come in all sizes, colors, and shapes. There are close to 20,000 types of butterflies. They are interesting to study!

A butterfly has a life cycle that is in four stages. The first stage is the egg stage, followed by the larva stage. The larva is a caterpillar, which eats as much as possible so it can grow into a butterfly. As the caterpillar grows, it loses its exoskeleton. This can happen several times. After a couple of weeks, the caterpillar enters the next stage, which is called the chrysalis. In the chrysalis stage, the caterpillar will become a butterfly.

Answer the following questions:

How many types of butterflies are there?
(20,000)   20,500

In what stage does the caterpillar become a butterfly?
first   (last)

How many stages of the butterfly life cycle are there?
(four)   six

Figure 7.27. A completed, modified activity using the Choose It strategy to aid a student in answering literal comprehension questions about an informational text.

19. Tell It With a Timeline

Students create a timeline of important events.

Student Goals

- Identify key events.
- Show the passage of time.
- Develop sequencing skills.

Directions for Teachers

1. Print a copy of the Tell It With a Timeline graphic organizer. (See Form 7 in Appendix B for a printable template.)
2. Identify a series of events that occurred over time. Use the student's life as an example, or take events from a story.
3. Review the event sequence.
4. Have the student complete the Tell It With a Timeline graphic organizer. The student can use text or illustrations, or give a verbal response.

Interventions

Scribe events for the student.

Use computer software to create the timeline.

Provide pictures for the student to place on the timeline.

Enlarge the timeline to give the student space to work.

Extensions

Encourage detailed descriptions of each event.

Have the student add more events to the timeline.

Remember

Use historical stories to reinforce understanding of a timeline.

Create a classroom timeline to encourage class participation.

Context for Student Work Sample

The work sample shown in Figure 7.28 illustrates how a student who works below grade level could work with a social studies assignment addressing the same content given to students working at grade level. Peers working within the fourth-grade curriculum have been learning and reviewing the California Gold Rush. Using the lesson materials and class notes, the

STRATEGIES FOR COMPREHENSION

student has been asked to show her understanding of the basic timeline of events. With the help of a paraprofessional, the student completed the assignment, which was modified by conceptual difficulty, educational goals, and instructional method.

Example: Tell It With a Timeline

Figure 7.28.   A completed, modified activity using the Tell It With a Timeline strategy to aid a student in representing historical events chronologically.

20. Read It

Students read grade-level content with the help of developmentally appropriate text.

Student Goals

- Recognize new vocabulary.
- Develop comprehension skills.

Directions for Teachers

1. Select a portion of grade-level content.
2. Rewrite the content using developmentally appropriate vocabulary. The vocabulary should be within the student's reading range.
3. Add visuals to support understanding of the text.
4. Preview the text with the student and identify any new vocabulary. Have the student read and discuss the text (with a teacher, peer, or paraprofessional) to develop understanding of the grade-level material.

Interventions

Provide pictures or symbols only.

Preteach vocabulary to improve understanding.

Enlarge the text or images for students with visual needs.

Extensions

Have the student create the modified text.

Increase the complexity of the text and concepts.

Have the student respond to comprehension questions about the text and/or images.

Remember

Providing concrete examples can support student understanding of new material. For instance, if the class is learning about the water cycle, a demonstration of the process can be useful.

Depending on the student's preference, placing modified content over the original content can help facilitate feelings of inclusion.

Context for Student Work Sample

The activity shown in Figure 7.29 depicts a portion of third-grade text that has been modified for a student who works below grade level. The text has been replaced with vocabulary that the student can read. Visuals that support the text have been added to further develop the student's understanding of the new concepts. This represents a modification of conceptual difficulty, educational goals, and instructional method.

Example: Read It

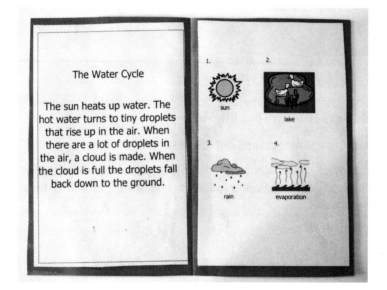

Figure 7.29. An example of a reading activity for which the Read It strategy has been used to make a text accessible to a student.

21. Sequence It

Students develop the ability to sequence materials, concepts, and numbers.

Student Goals

- Develop the ability to sort.

- Develop the ability to sequence content according to predetermined criteria (e.g., sequence events in chronological order).

- Develop the ability to prioritize.

Directions for Teachers

1. Use a grade-level activity with a series of numbers, letters, or materials.

2. Determine the sequencing criteria based on the student's IEP goals. For instance, the student can sequence based on size, location, sound, or physical attributes.

3. Have students sequence the material. For instance, the student can sequence numbers from big to small.

Interventions

Use a number line if the student is sequencing numbers.

Use prompts to support the sequencing of text. Prompts, such as using the first letter of the word or the first couple of letters of the word, can cue student response.

Have a peer scribe the answer(s).

Reduce the amount of material to sequence.

Extensions

Increase the amount of material to be sequenced.

Increase the complexity of material to be sequenced. For example, rather than sequencing numbers from big to small, the student can sequence objects by height.

Remember

This activity works well for groups of students.

Give the student a choice in the materials to sequence, the criteria for sequencing, and any tools used to sequence (e.g., a yardstick or tape measure used to sequence objects according to height).

Context for Student Work Sample

The activity and work sample shown in Figures 7.30 and 7.31 show how a student who works below grade level in mathematics can meet his IEP goal using the same material that his typically developing peers are working on. The fourth-grade class has been learning to round

STRATEGIES FOR COMPREHENSION

large numbers, as shown in Figure 7.30. While peers work on rounding, the student uses the same numbers to work on his goal to develop sequencing skills, as shown in Figure 7.31. For each question, instead of rounding the large number, the student writes the digits within that number in sequence, from largest to smallest (e.g., sequencing the digits within 65,733 as 7, 6, 5, 3, 3). This represents a modification of conceptual difficulty, educational goals, and instructional method.

Example: Sequence It

Name: _____   Date: _____

Grade 3 Math
Rounding Numbers

1. Round to the nearest hundred: 65,733 _____

2. Round to the nearest ten: 762 _____

3. Round to the nearest ten: 8,936 _____

4. Round to the nearest hundred: 76,256 _____

5. Round to the nearest hundred: 937 _____

Figure 7.30. An example of an activity with which the Sequence It strategy could be used.

Name: *Michael* _____   Date: *2/7/16* _____

Grade 3 Math
Rounding Numbers

1. ~~Round to the nearest hundred:~~ 65,733 *76533*

2. ~~Round to the nearest ten:~~ 762 *762*

3. ~~Round to the nearest ten:~~ 8,936 *9863*

4. ~~Round to the nearest hundred:~~ 76,256 *76652*

5. ~~Round to the nearest hundred:~~ 937 *973*

Figure 7.31. A completed, modified activity using the Sequence It strategy to give a student practice with mathematics skills appropriate to his developmental level.

22. Make It

Students can represent their knowledge and understanding of concepts by creating a representation.

Student Goals

- Make a representation of a concept.
- Demonstrate understanding of a concept.
- Develop planning skills.

Directions for Teachers

1. Identify the most important concept related to a topic that is relevant and familiar to the student.
2. Review understanding of the concept.
3. Have the student decide on a way to represent his or her understanding of the concept. For example, the student can illustrate, create a presentation, build a model, or write about the concept. Discuss possible criteria to be included in the activity.
4. Help the student gather and use appropriate materials to complete the assignment.

Interventions

Prompt and provide cues to support student understanding of text.

Predetermine the most appropriate way for the student to represent understanding.

Reduce the complexity of the concept the student is to represent. For instance, if the student is learning about habitats, have the student create a representation of an animal.

Extensions

Have the student provide a written or verbal description of the representation.

Have the student work with a partner to create the representation of the concept.

Encourage the student to present it to the class or a small group.

Remember

Have the student complete the assignment with as much independence as possible.

Context for Student Work Sample

The work sample shown in Figure 7.32 shows how a student who works below grade level can meet an IEP-related standard that is within the same science strand that his typically developing peers are working on. The fourth-grade class has been learning and working with

STRATEGIES FOR COMPREHENSION

information on ecosystems. The student with an IEP has a modified assignment that requires him to create a model of a forest habitat. With the help of his parents at home, the student has created a diorama of a pond habitat.

Example: Make It

Figure 7.32. An example of the Make It strategy; this student built a diorama depicting his understanding of habitats.

23. I Know It. I Learned It.

This strategy is based on the well-known strategy called *K-W-L* (Know, Want to Know, Learned; Ogle, 1986). It is modified to elicit direct responses from students prior to and after an activity or lesson.

Student Goals

- Recall knowledge.

- Summarize information.

- Integrate new knowledge.

- Develop the ability to focus on new information.

Directions for Teachers

1. Print a copy of the I Know It. I Learned It graphic organizer. (See Form 8 in Appendix B for a printable template.)

2. Prior to the start of a new unit of study, have the student identify things he or she knows about the topic.

3. Have the student complete the first column (*I Know*) in the graphic organizer.

4. During the unit of study, review new concepts with students to ensure understanding.

5. At the end of the unit, have the student complete the second column (*I Learned*) on the graphic organizer.

Interventions

Activate prior knowledge by reading or discussing the topic prior to its introduction.

Have the student complete only one of the columns on the graphic organizer.

If the student has issues with written output, use images to illustrate the student's responses.

Extensions

Have the student compare answers with other students' answers in a whole-class activity.

Have the student combine both sections to create a report. The type of report can depend on the student's ability and interest. It can be an oral report or a written report; it can be an individual or group report.

Insert a third column (between the first and the second), and have the student generate questions he or she may have about the topic before studying it.

STRATEGIES FOR COMPREHENSION

Remember

This activity can be done as a whole class or in groups.

Ensure that the student feels comfortable sharing his or her knowledge, particularly if working with a group.

Context for Student Work Sample

The work sample shown in Figure 7.33 illustrates how an eighth-grade student working below grade level can respond to a science lesson on food webs. The teacher has asked the student to focus on researching an animal within a food web. Prior to researching the chosen animal, the bear, the student listed what he knew about bears on the left hand side of the chart. Once the research was completed (by reading nonfiction text and watching videos), the student then listed what new facts he had learned. The assignment shown has been modified in content, concept, educational goals, and instructional method.

Example: I Know It. I Learned It.

Name: _Jose_____   Date: _12/11/17_____

I Know It. I Learned It.

Topic: Bears	
I Know	I Learned
• Bears are big. • Bears are brown and black. • Bears eat meat. • Bears sleep in winter.	• Bears eat plants and fish. • Bears can run faster than people. • Bears live all over the world. • A panda bear is not a bear.

Figure 7.33. A completed, modified activity using the I Know It. I Learned It. strategy to help a student work with concepts related to the grade-level science curriculum.

24. Cut It Out

Students create a picture collage of items related to the lesson.

Student Goals

- Develop classification skills.

- Select accurate information.

- Develop the ability to follow directions.

Directions for Teachers

1. Identify and review key concepts in the lesson.

2. Gather old magazines, brochures, posters, or any other illustration that can be cut out and used in a collage.

3. Set a list of criteria for the items that you want the student to find. For example, if the class is learning about the state of California, the student might look for things such as oranges, beaches, and Disneyland.

4. Have the student find and cut out images that are related to the lesson. Ask the student to affix images to a background (e.g., poster board, construction paper) to create a collage of images related to the lesson.

Interventions

Cut out images ahead of time for the student to use.

Limit the number of images the student is to collect.

A peer, paraprofessional, or teacher can support the selection process.

Have the student work with a peer to complete the activity.

Extensions

The criteria for the collage can be complex.

The student can determine a topic for the activity.

The student can work with a peer to complete the activity.

Remember

Provide the student with a number of sources to use to find images, such as magazines, newspapers, old calendars, or online stock photo sites. Be sure to preview the sources first!

Context for Student Work Sample

The work sample shown in Figure 7.34 depicts a collage of pictures of items that are orange. The student who completed this collage is learning an IEP-related goal that requires her to know her basic colors. While her third-grade classmates were learning how to classify rocks based on color and shape, she classified pictures by color. She found pictures that met the classification criterion, orange, in magazines and online. With the help of a paraprofessional, she created a simple collage of pictures of orange items. This represents a modification of content, conceptual difficulty, educational goals, and instructional method.

Example: Cut It Out

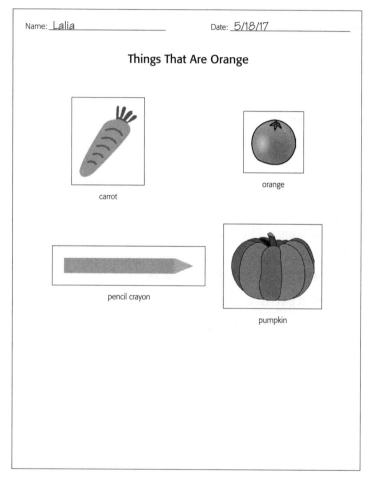

Figure 7.34. An example of a student-made collage used with the Cut It Out strategy. Creating the collage gives the student practice with classifying.

25. Draw It

Students demonstrate understanding of new material through illustration.

Student Goals

- Depict understanding of new material.

- Summarize the main idea.

- Develop artistic skills.

Directions for Teachers

1. Have student recall the main idea or key concept of the lesson.

2. Have the student illustrate the main idea to demonstrate understanding.

3. For follow-up, have the student describe the illustration.

Interventions

Reteach the lesson to identify the main idea and provide follow-up discussion to ensure understanding of the main idea. The student can also work with peers to determine the main idea of the lesson.

Predetermine the main idea that the student will work with.

Have the student work with a partner to illustrate the main idea.

Provide the most appropriate method for the illustration. For example, the student can use software, pencil and paper, paint, or modeling clay.

Extensions

Have the student include a written or verbal description of the illustration.

Encourage the student to add as much detail as possible to the illustration.

Remember

Provide students with a choice in how they would like to illustrate the main idea.

Context for Student Work Sample

The work sample shown in Figure 7.35 depicts how a student can respond to an English language arts assignment given to her third-grade class. Both the student and her peers read a brief informational passage about nurses; her peers are required to determine the main idea of the passage and write it in their own words. (See the passage and directions in the top half of Figure 7.35.) While her peers paraphrase the main idea in the text, the student is asked to illustrate the main idea. This represents a modification of conceptual difficulty, educational goals, and instructional method.

Example: Draw It

> **Read the following to determine the main idea. Rewrite it in your own words.**
>
> There are various jobs in a hospital. Some jobs are more stressful than others, whereas others bring joy and satisfaction. Nurses have a job that can be stressful but brings great satisfaction. Nurses work with people who are sick or injured. The job of the nurse is to help the patient heal and go back to living their life. They give the patient medicine that is ordered by the doctor. They make sure the patient is comfortable. If this type of job interests you, you might want to consider a career in nursing.

Name: May

Figure 7.35. A completed, modified activity using the Draw It strategy to provide a student with a way to represent the main idea of an informational passage.

26. Cloze It

Students demonstrate understanding of concepts by reading a passage with some portions of text omitted and supplying the missing content.

Student Goals

- Distinguish the correct answer from a list of choices.
- Develop comprehension skills.
- Develop prediction skills.

Directions for Teachers

1. Determine the purpose of the cloze activity by using the goals of the student's IEP. For example, will the cloze be used to develop understanding of a concept, build vocabulary, or practice letter sounds?
2. Using a portion of text from the class activity, recreate it either on paper or in digital format.
3. Omit words related to the student's learning outcomes, so that filling in the words will support these outcomes.
4. Encourage the student to read the text and complete the cloze activity.

Interventions

Provide a word bank from which the student can choose answers.

Reread the text with the student to ensure understanding.

Provide letter clues to prompt the student's response.

Use visuals in the place of text.

Extensions

Increase the complexity of text.

Increase the length of text.

Increase the number of cloze responses required.

Remember

Ensure that students understand how to complete a cloze assignment. Model the process if necessary, showing the student how to check the answer for suitability.

Context for Student Work Sample

The work sample shown in Figure 7.36 illustrates how a student could work on her IEP-related goal of building comprehension skills. Peers are working on a sixth-grade comprehension activity related to a novel they are reading. They are providing written answers to questions about the first three chapters. Meanwhile, the teacher provides a more appropriate comprehension assignment in the form of a cloze activity for the student to complete. The teacher provides sentences and includes an answer bank for the student to refer to while completing the assignment. This represents a modification of conceptual difficulty, educational goals, and instructional method.

Example: Cloze It

Name: _Alex_   Date: _11/21/17_

Sight Words

I go to _sleep_ at night.

The grass is _green_.

We like to _read_ books.

Dinner is at _____ o'clock.

We _____ the dishes after dinner.

I sing a _____ when I am happy.

song	read	sleep
five	wash	green

Figure 7.36. A completed, modified activity using the Cloze It strategy.

27. Tell Me a Story About It

Students create a story involving a concept or other informational material learned in class.

Student Goals

- Integrate knowledge of story structure.

- Edit errors.

- Develop creativity skills.

Directions for Teachers

1. Print a copy of the Tell Me a Story About It graphic organizer. (See Form 9 in Appendix B for a printable template.)

2. Have the student identify a topic and storyline that ties in with the lesson material.

3. Use the student's IEP goals and prior knowledge to determine the level of detail and structure that should be included in the story. (*Note:* The graphic organizer uses a basic story structure that can be altered according to the student's abilities and learning goals.)

4. Provide the student with the Tell Me a Story About It graphic organizer to fill out.

5. Encourage the student to edit and revise the story where necessary. (Giving the student a checklist of edits to make is helpful.)

6. The student can transcribe the story from the graphic organizer into a final format, such as a written paragraph or audio recording.

Interventions

Scribe the story for the student.

Have the student use images to represent what happens in the story.

The student can work with a peer to complete the story.

Reduce the complexity of the story structure with which the student is expected to work.

Extensions

Increase the length and complexity of the story the student is asked to develop.

Have the student illustrate the story.

Have the student share the story in a way that is appropriate to his or her ability level. For example, if the student does not speak, the story can be typed into a text-to-speech software program or app.

Remember

The story can be conveyed in a variety of formats, depending on the student's interests and abilities. For example, a student with dysgraphia might choose to type the story in a Word document on the computer or create an audio recording of the story

Context for Student Work Sample

The work sample shown in Figure 7.37 illustrates how a third-grade student writing below grade level could learn simple story structure related to the grade-level curriculum and to the student's IEP goals. Peers working within the grade-level curriculum are learning how to write narratives and use temporal words to signal event order. This student uses a graphic organizer with prewritten transitional words to record the order of events that occurred in a simple narrative. This assignment represents a modification of conceptual difficulty, educational goals, and instructional method.

Example: Tell Me a Story About It

Name: Ruben   Date: 1/13/18

Tell Me a Story About It

First, the boy was walking his dog in the park.

Then, the boy dropped the leash.

Finally, the dog ran away.

Figure 7.37. A completed, modified activity using the Tell Me a Story About It strategy to provide a student with practice using temporal words to relate a simple sequence of events.

STRATEGIES FOR COMPREHENSION

28. Put It in a Flowchart

Students write a sequence of events or the steps of a process using a flowchart.

Student Goals

- Organize information.
- Follow directions.
- Develop sequencing skills.

Directions for Teachers

1. Print a copy of the Put It in a Flowchart graphic organizer. (See Form 10 in Appendix B for a printable template.)
2. Identify an event or process related to the class lesson that involves a series of steps to complete.
3. Ask the student to recall how the event unfolded or recall the order of steps to complete a process.
4. Have the student use the Put It in a Flowchart graphic organizer to convey the activity information.

Interventions

Ensure that the student understands the purpose of a flowchart and how it is read.

Provide pictures or symbols for the student to use.

Enlarge the graphic organizer.

Have prewritten sentences available (e.g., prewritten sentences on sentence strips) for the student to use in the flowchart.

Extensions

Ask the student to create a flowchart using his or her own selected topic.

Have the student create a flowchart of steps for another person to use.

Introduce the different symbols used in more complex flowcharts. For example, a diamond shape indicates a question that is asked in the process.

Remember

Flowcharts can also be used in developing appropriate social and/or emotional behavior in students. For example, flowcharts can be used to list a sequence of events to help students understand a class routine or class expectation. A teacher might create a flowchart for handing in homework (i.e., take homework out of backpack → make sure name is on homework → put homework in the tray on the teacher's desk). Alternatively, a flowchart can be made for illustrating a social situation. For example, a flowchart outlining how to greet another person might be helpful for a student with Asperger syndrome (i.e., look the other person in the eye → smile → say "Hello").

Context for Student Work Sample

The work sample shown in Figure 7.38 illustrates how a fourth-grade student who works below grade level can learn from the grade-level science curriculum. Peers working within the grade-level curriculum are learning about ecosystems and the relationship between living things and their environment. At the same time, this student's IEP team has set a goal that the student will learn two key concepts related to this curriculum unit. The assignment shown has the student identifying one of those concepts—namely, how the sun affects animals and plants. This assignment represents a modification of conceptual difficulty, educational goals, and instructional method.

Example: Put It in a Flowchart

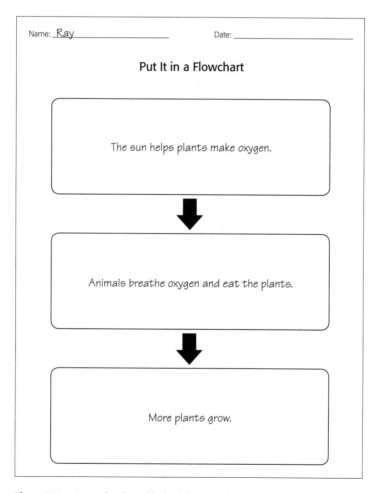

Figure 7.38. A completed, modified activity using the Put It in a Flowchart strategy to allow a student to work in a developmentally appropriate way with concepts from the grade-level curriculum.

29. Note It

Students learn to note key ideas about new concepts.

Student Goals

- Organize ideas.

- Summarize ideas.

- Develop comprehension skills.

Directions for Teachers

1. Print a copy of the Note It graphic organizer. (See Form 11 in Appendix B for a printable template.)

2. Review the lesson with the student, using lesson notes, visuals, or discussion. Have the student identify a key or big idea of the lesson. The teacher can help the student respond by asking the student what the lesson was about or what the purpose of the lesson was. The student may be able to do this independently or may require prompting. Highlighting the main idea in a text is a helpful way of distinguishing it from details.

3. Have the student use the Note It graphic organizer to complete the lesson.

4. In the left-hand column (*Topic*), have the student record a key idea of the lesson (e.g., *pharaohs* would be a key concept in a lesson on Egyptian civilization). Depending on the student's ability level, the student can write or use a symbol to represent his or her answer.

5. In the right-hand column (*Big Ideas About the Topic*), have the student list what he or she has learned in relation to the key concept learned during the lesson. The student can use lesson notes or visuals for support in remembering and recording the answers, or have a peer provide support. A highlighter in a different color can be used to mark the student's answers. The student can list as many answers as appropriate.

6. Review the notes with the student, or have the student share his or her notes with peers.

Interventions

Have the student use images instead of words to note details related to the key concept.

Give prompts or cues to help the student take notes.

Have the student give verbal responses to note details related to the key concept.

Extensions

Encourage the student to provide increasingly specific details, such as names, dates, and/or locations.

Have the student highlight important vocabulary words and learn the definitions.

Ask the student to complete more note-taking sheets related to the topic in order to enhance understanding of the class lesson.

Remember

If the student has completed several note-taking sheets on the same curriculum unit, the notes can be compiled to create a report or review of the unit. Simply collect notes and assemble in a folder for the student (or scan for use on the computer). Alternatively, depending on the student's ability level, the student can create a summary of the unit using the notes. The student can use the notes to write a summary of each key concept in the unit, which would involve putting each detail into a sentence. He or she may be able to do this independently or with support (e.g., a checklist for the sequence of steps required to create the report), or the student may need a scribe.

Students can record notes through word processing, speech-to-text software, or voice recording.

Context for Student Work Sample

The work sample shown in Figure 7.39 illustrates how a sixth-grade student working below grade level could learn content related to the grade-level curriculum and to her IEP goals. The class has been learning about Egyptian civilization. Peers respond to each lesson by answering a series of comprehension questions (not shown here). In the meantime, the student is asked to respond to the lesson about Egyptian civilization at the level appropriate to her development. In this example, she is asked to note the importance of the pharaohs and then use the right side of the organizer to provide information about this key concept. This assignment represents a modification of conceptual difficulty, educational goals, and instructional method.

Example: Note It

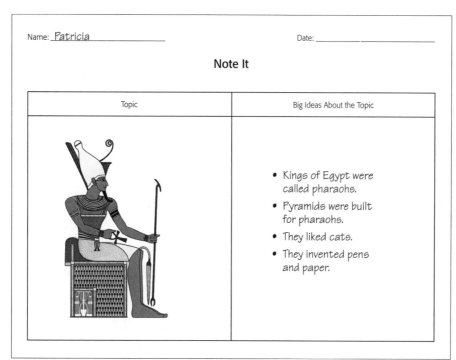

Figure 7.39. A completed, modified activity using the Note It strategy to allow a student to take notes on concepts from the grade-level curriculum in a developmentally appropriate way.

30. Report It

Students report on the elements of a story they have read.

Student Goals

- Recall story elements such as character, setting, and events.

- Summarize ideas.

- Demonstrate comprehension skills.

Directions for Teachers

1. Print a copy of the Report It graphic organizer. (See Form 12 in Appendix B for a printable template.). Note that this template can be altered and modified according to the ability and IEP goals of the student. This particular template is a more challenging version of the Detail It strategy, in which students are asked to provide only details about the *where, when,* and *who* in the story. For this particular strategy, students are not only asked about character and setting, but they are also asked to give an overview of the beginning, middle, and end of the book.

2. Have the student read or listen to a developmentally appropriate story.

3. Have the student recall and record elements of the story, with support as needed. The activity can be completed while reading the story or when the story has been finished.

Interventions

Have the student use images instead of words to represent the elements of the story (e.g., characters, setting, plot events).

Give student prompts or clues to help them recall information.

Scribe the student's responses.

Reduce the amount of information the student is expected to provide.

Extensions

Encourage the student to provide details.

Have the student create an illustration to accompany the report.

Remember

This is an activity suitable for all students in the class. Depending on the student's interests and abilities, the report can be completed in various ways. For example, a student with challenges that affect the production of written output might use word processing software on the computer or speech-to-text software.

Context for Student Work Sample

The work sample shown in Figure 7.40 illustrates how a seventh-grade student working below grade level could learn content related to the grade-level curriculum and to the student's IEP goals. Students in the class have been reading novels of their choice; they are learning to describe how their story's plot unfolds in a series of episodes, as well as how the characters respond or change as the plot moves toward a resolution. This student has chosen John Reynolds Gardiner's *Stone Fox,* which is within her range of reading ability (approximately third grade). She is learning a more developmentally appropriate standard from the same English language arts strand, which is to describe characters in a story and explain how their actions contribute to the sequence of events. The student has been given a modified version of the grade-level class activity and was asked to recount the characters in the story and the major plot events, including which characters were central to the plot events. This assignment represents a modification of content, conceptual difficulty, educational goals, and instructional method.

Example: Report It

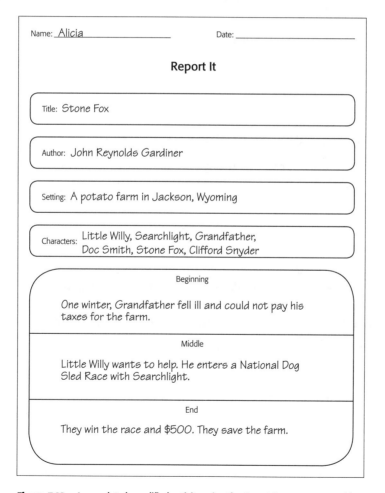

Figure 7.40. A completed, modified activity using the Report It strategy to provide a student practice in understanding story elements and the relationships among them using a developmentally appropriate text.

31. Web It

Students create a graphic representation of their knowledge and ideas related to a topic.

Student Goals

- Demonstrate relationships between ideas.
- Depict understanding of a topic.
- Summarize information.

Directions for Teachers

1. Choose a concept from the class activity that is familiar to the student and aligns with the student's IEP goals.

2. Ask the student to form a concept map. This is a graphic representation of the knowledge and ideas a student has about a topic.

3. Have the student create categories for the topic. For instance:

(Arrows can be used to show the relationship between ideas.)

4. Encourage the student to create as many categories and subcategories as possible.

Interventions

Simplify the complexity of the topic.

Use concrete materials, such as plastic nesting containers, to demonstrate the relationship between concepts. For example, for a lesson on basic geography concepts, the largest container can represent Earth; the second largest container can represent a continent on Earth; the third largest would represent a country, and so forth.

Reduce the amount of knowledge expected from the student.

Scribe for the student.

Use images instead of words on the concept map.

Extensions

Increase the complexity of the concept.

Increase the number of categories expected from the student.

Create a concept map to which the whole class can contribute.

Remember

There are many different types of software and web sites where the student can create concept maps. A popular online program is MindMeister (www.mindmeister.com).

Give the students a choice of the tools they would like to use to create the concept map.

Context for Student Work Sample

The work sample shown in Figure 7.41 illustrates how a student who writes well below grade level could work with a written assignment given to the general education class. Tenth-grade peers are writing narratives about either real or imaginary experiences, using well-chosen details. Similarly, the student has chosen to convey information about her love for summer. She uses a web to record the details about summer that she loves. This assignment represents a modification of conceptual difficulty, educational goals, and instructional method.

Example: Web It

Figure 7.41. An example of a concept map that was created using the Web It strategy; creating the concept map in lieu of writing a personal narrative allowed the student to represent details of a meaningful experience.

32. Collect It

Students can represent their knowledge of a topic or concept through a collection of related artifacts.

Student Goals

- Identify the relationship between artifacts and topic.

- Integrate knowledge with real-world materials.

- Develop presentation skills.

Directions

1. Have the student select a topic of interest related to the curriculum and aligned with his or her IEP goals.

2. Have the student identify artifacts that will represent his or her knowledge of the topic.

3. Ask the student to collect the artifacts and describe their relation to the topic.

Interventions

Preselect a topic for the student.

Have the student select images to represent artifacts.

Limit the number of artifacts the student collects.

Scribe the student's description of artifacts.

Extensions

Have the student describe the artifacts. Depending on the student's ability level, he or she can use an appropriate writing tool (such as an iPad, a computer, or a pencil and paper) to record a few words or a sentence (or more) describing each artifact.

Have the student present the artifacts to the class.

Remember

The whole class can participate in this activity.

Context for Student Work Sample

The work sample shown in Figure 7.42 depicts ocean-related items collected by a student. The student's second-grade class is learning mapping skills by naming the oceans and continents of the world. To help develop the student's understanding of oceans, the student has collected several artifacts found in the ocean. This represents a modification of conceptual difficulty, educational goals, and instructional method.

Example: Collect It

Figure 7.42. An example of the Collect It strategy; this student collected and discussed items to represent knowledge of the concept of oceans.

33. Chart It

Students can create a T-chart to sort and/or connect ideas as well as information.

Student Goals

- Sort information.
- Understand relationships between concepts.
- Organize a response.

Directions for Teachers

1. Print a copy of the Chart It graphic organizer. (See Form 13 in Appendix B for a printable template.)

2. Determine the lesson-related criteria for the T-chart. Ensure that the criteria align with the student's IEP goals.

3. Demonstrate how the student can record a word or idea on the left-hand side of the chart. On the right-hand side of the chart, the student can record a correlating idea. For example, the student might be learning about presidents of the United States. On the left side of the chart, he can name a president, and on the right side of the chart, he can record the dates of that individual's presidency.

4. Have the student use lesson-related materials and peer and/or teacher support to complete the chart.

Interventions

Scribe the student's responses.

Give prompts or cues to help the student sort answers.

Give the student pictures to choose from, and have the student glue them onto the correct side of the chart.

Have the student give verbal responses that address the relationships between ideas.

Extensions

Provide more complex criteria or a more complex topic with which to work.

Increase the number of student responses expected.

Remember

This graphic organizer is a great tool for organizing important ideas and facts. It can be a helpful study tool for all students.

Context for Student Work Sample

The work sample shown in Figure 7.43 illustrates how a student who works below grade level could work with social studies content assigned in fifth grade. Peers working within the grade-level curriculum are labeling the states and corresponding capitals on a map of the United States. For this student, the assignment has been modified. She was given a written list of five states and five capital cities. She sorted and listed the states and their corresponding capital cities in the T-chart. This represents a modification of conceptual difficulty, educational goals, and instructional method.

Example: Chart It

Name: _Renee_   Date: _7/22/17_

Chart It

State	Capital
California	Sacramento
Washington	Olympia
Idaho	Boise
Texas	Austin
Arizona	Phoenix

Figure 7.43. A completed, modified activity using the Chart It strategy to provide a student a means of representing her knowledge of state capitals.

34. Match It

Students distinguish and match vocabulary in this strategy.

Student Goals

- Identify similarities and differences.
- Develop number or word recognition skills.
- Sort information and/or ideas.

Directions for Teachers

1. Print or type vocabulary from the lesson.
2. Create a duplicate list.
3. Have students review the vocabulary on the list.
4. Ask the student to match the vocabulary words.

Interventions

Offer prompts or cues to initiate student responses.

Reduce the complexity of the assignment.

Reduce the number of words to match.

Use concrete items to match instead of ideas.

Extensions

Increase the number of words to match.

Increase the complexity of words to be matched.

Have students match images or numbers instead of vocabulary.

Remember

This strategy can easily become a game of Memory for students to play with peers. Write the words students are to match on index cards (two cards for each word). Students can place the cards face down. Each student takes a turn flipping two cards over to find a match. If the cards are not matched, they are put face down again. Students try to remember which cards can be flipped over and result in a match.

Context for Student Work Sample

The work sample shown in Figure 7.44 illustrates how a third-grade student working below grade level could learn content related to the grade-level science curriculum and to the student's IEP goals. Peers working within the grade-level curriculum are learning about bodies of water on Earth. Relatedly, this student's IEP team has set a goal that the student will learn four new vocabulary words related to water. The assignment shown involves matching the new vocabulary words. This represents a modification of conceptual difficulty, educational goals, and instructional method.

Example: Match It

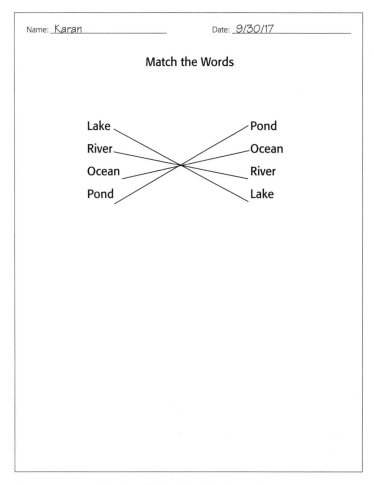

Figure 7.44. A completed, modified activity using the Match It strategy.

35. Compare It and Contrast It

Students use a graphic organizer to compare and contrast two concepts.

Student Goals

- Identify similarities and differences.
- Develop the ability to make decisions.
- Locate information.

Directions for Teachers

1. Print a copy of the Compare It and Contrast It graphic organizer. (See Form 14 in Appendix B for a printable template.)

2. Review the class lesson with the student and identify two related events or concepts. For example, if the class is learning about the human body, the student can compare and contrast arms and legs.

3. Activate prior knowledge by discussing things that are the same and different between the two related concepts.

4. Ensure that the student is familiar with Venn diagrams and how they are used. The teacher can review by using concrete objects such as toy hoops. The hoops can be placed on the floor and overlapped. Items such as shoes can be used to demonstrate how a Venn diagram can help the student compare and contrast information. For example, white shoes can be placed in the left hoop, black shoes can be placed in the right hoop, and shoes that are black and white can be placed where the hoops overlap.

5. Have the student use the Compare It and Contrast It graphic organizer to demonstrate understanding of the similarities and differences between the topics.

Interventions

Limit the number of responses expected from the student.

Scribe the student's responses.

Use pictures or symbols to represent answers.

Enlarge the template for accessibility.

Have prewritten sentences available for the student to use and sort into the appropriate categories.

Extensions

Have the student create a written summary of similarities and differences between the two concepts.

Ask the student to provide more detail in his or her responses.

Remember

Students can share their responses with one another.

Context for Student Work Sample

The work sample shown in Figure 7.45 illustrates how a fourth-grade student reading below grade level could learn content related to the grade-level curriculum and to the student's IEP goals. Together, the class is reading *Shiloh,* by Phyllis Reynolds Naylor. Peers are working on comparing and contrasting the way Judd Travers and Marty Preston think animals should be treated. Meanwhile, the student completes a related compare/contrast activity by comparing and contrasting dogs and cats. The assignment shown involves modifications to content, conceptual difficulty, educational goals, and instructional method.

Example: Compare It and Contrast It

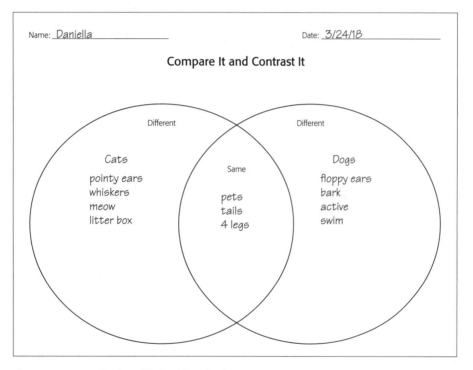

Figure 7.45. A completed, modified activity using the strategy, Compare It and Contrast It, to give the student practice comparing concepts related to the grade-level curriculum.

36. Group It

Students can group related concepts, words, objects, and/or numbers using this strategy.

Student Goals

- See patterns and similarities.
- Develop classifying skills.
- Develop decision-making skills.

Directions for Teachers

1. Select numbers, words, or concepts from the main lesson.
2. Create durable cards using the numbers, words, or concepts.
3. Give the student criteria for grouping the cards.
4. Have the student complete the activity.

Interventions

Substitute words and numbers for images.

Give the student concrete items to group, such as shapes, school supplies, foods, or toys.

Reduce the number or items to group.

Extensions

Ask the student to classify words related to a topic of interest. For example, if the student is interested in cars, he or she can group passenger cars and nonpassenger cars.

Add the words to a vocabulary bank for the student to learn.

Remember

Grouping activities can be done with all grades from kindergarten to high school.

Context for Student Work Sample

The work sample shown in Figure 7.46 illustrates how a fourth-grade student working below grade level could learn content related to the grade-level science curriculum and to the student's IEP goals. Peers working within the grade-level curriculum are learning about circulation and respiration in animals. Relatedly, this student's IEP team has set a goal that the student will develop classification skills. The assignment shown involves sorting animals that live on land and animals that spend most of their life in or near water. This represents a modification of content, conceptual difficulty, educational goals, and instructional method.

Example: Group It

Figure 7.46. An example of the Group It strategy used to give the student practice with categorizing. (Contributed by Kristen Eredics.)

37. Edit It

Students learn to identify and revise errors.

Student Goals

- Activate prior knowledge.
- Learn to recognize errors.
- Correct errors.
- Refine work for accuracy.

Directions for Teachers

1. Predetermine the type of errors on which the student should focus, such as checking the spelling of a familiar word.

2. Prewrite developmentally appropriate sentences that contain spelling errors. Model the process of identifying spelling errors in an activity (e.g., circle the error).

3. Provide guided practice. Teachers may want to gradually expand the types of errors the student should look for (e.g., errors in the use of capital letters and punctuation). Teachers can also create a checklist of the types of errors students should look for.

4. Have the student complete an editing activity independently.

Interventions

Have the student edit his or her work with the help of a peer.

During guided practice, reduce the complexity of the word or the sentence the student edits.

Extensions

Increase the number of different types of errors that the student is to look for.

Have the student use different ways of marking the error, depending on the type of error.

Remember

This strategy can be used with the whole class.

Context for Student Work Sample

The activity and work sample shown in Figure 7.47 illustrate how a fifth-grade student working below grade level could learn a writing standard taken from the CCSS. With guidance and support, peers are developing and strengthening writing as needed by planning, revising, editing, rewriting, or trying a new approach. The student is also learning the process of editing written work. The assignment shown involves the student identifying spelling errors in a series of simple sentences. This represents a modification of conceptual difficulty, educational goals, and instructional method.

Example: Edit It

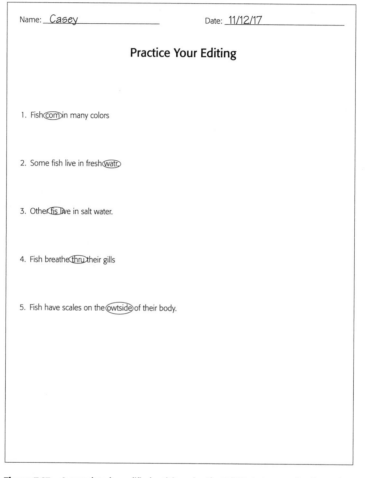

Figure 7.47. A completed, modified activity using the Edit It strategy to give the student developmentally appropriate practice with one stage of the writing process.

38. Judge It for Yourself

Students use a Judge It for Yourself graphic organizer to help them make a decision.

Student Goals

- Understand cause-and-effect relationships
- Develop decision-making skills based on evidence.

Directions for Teachers

1. Print a copy of the Judge It for Yourself graphic organizer. (See Form 15 in Appendix B for a printable template.)

2. Review the student's understanding of the words *cause* and *effect*. Explain that these words help people understand why things happen.

3. Demonstrate cause and effect using concrete examples. Some ideas include turning a light switch on and off, creating a row of dominoes and pushing the first domino in the row, or building a tower of blocks and removing a block at the very bottom. Furthermore, the teacher can discuss real-life examples related to common day-to-day activities, such as turning the key to start a car engine or using a match to light a candle.

4. Name an event or action related to the class lesson that ties into the student's IEP goals.

5. Use the Judge It for Yourself graphic organizer to explain the cause and the effect of the event or action.

6. Have the student complete the activity.

Interventions

Provide pictures or symbols for the student to use.

Predetermine a topic for the student.

Enlarge the template for accessibility.

Have prewritten sentences for the students to use and sort.

Extensions

Give the student a sentence and ask him or her to determine which part of the sentence is the cause and which part is the effect.

Ask the student to create a sentence about the cause and effect he or she identified.

STRATEGIES FOR KNOWLEDGE UTILIZATION

Remember

Use concepts and reading material that are at the student's level.

This strategy can be done with a small group of students.

This strategy can also be applied to social stories that support behavior.

Context for Student Work Sample

The work sample shown in Figure 7.48 illustrates how a ninth-grade student working below grade level could learn content related to the grade-level health education curriculum. The class has been asked to explain how decisions regarding health behaviors have consequences for oneself and others. While peers respond by writing about a time they made a decision that affected their health, the student completes a cause-and-effect activity that also reviews a decision he made and the consequences of that decision. The activity has been modified by conceptual difficulty, educational goals, and instructional method.

Example: Judge It for Yourself

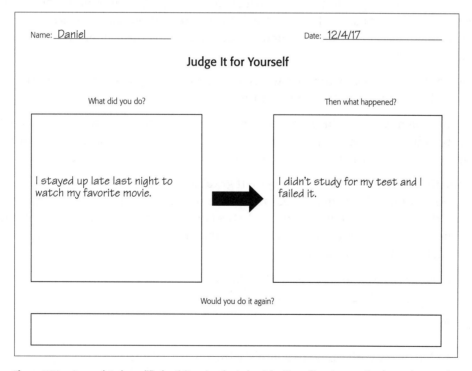

Figure 7.48. A completed, modified activity using the Judge It for Yourself strategy to give the student practice identifying the consequences of a decision.

STRATEGIES FOR KNOWLEDGE UTILIZATION

39. Investigate It

Students investigate to find out about a topic that interests them.

Student Goals

- Learn new information.
- Represent ideas.
- Summarize information.

Directions for Teachers

1. Print a copy of the Investigate It graphic organizer. (See Form 16 in Appendix B for a printable template.)

2. Note that this activity may take some time to complete. The process of finding the relevant information and recording it is just as important as the final product. In addition, this activity may require a lot of direct support and guidance, depending on the ability level of the student. Modeling the information-gathering process and showing the student an example of a completed report can provide the student with a concrete explanation of the activity.

3. Have the student choose a topic on which to report. The topic can be related to a unit of study in the classroom or to a topic of interest.

4. Give the student an opportunity to use developmentally appropriate resources to locate and collect information about the topic, with support when necessary. For example, the student can find information online, in the library, or by talking with an expert.

5. Provide the student with the Investigate It graphic organizer. Have the student complete one section of the graphic organizer at a time. The student must understand what information he or she needs to find, locate the correct information, and record it in the corresponding information box. For further support, provide the student with prompts to complete each information box.

6. The student can add illustrations and diagrams where suitable.

Interventions

Have the student work with a peer to complete the investigation.

Provide resources and information about the topic for the student.

Provide images for the student to use.

Scribe the student's responses.

Enlarge the graphic organizer.

Have prewritten sentences for the students to use and organize into a report.

Extensions

Have the student make a trivia game about the topic.

Have the student present the investigation about the topic to the class. This can be done orally or through the use of audiovisual aids.

Remember

Encourage the student to be creative with the report. Add music, a live demonstration, or photographs to enhance audience interest.

This activity is suitable for all students.

Context for Student Work Sample

The work sample shown in Figure 7.49 illustrates how a sixth-grade student working below grade level could learn content related to the grade-level curriculum. The class has been learning about Earth's features and plate tectonics. Relatedly, the student investigates one of her favorite topics in Earth Science—volcanoes. The activity has been modified by content, conceptual difficulty, educational goals, and instructional method.

Example: Investigate It

Investigate It

Topic: Volcanoes

Report by: Mariana

Date: 5/22/18

1. What is it?

A volcano is a hole in the ground.
It lets hot rocks escape from under the ground.

2. Tell me about it.

The hot rocks underground are called magma.
The land can pull apart and the hot rocks can come out of the hole.
When the hot rocks come out it is called lava.
Lava can burn forests.
There are volcanoes under the water.
There are volcanoes on other planets like Jupiter.

3. Why do you like it?

Volcanoes can change the way the earth looks.

4. Where did you get your information from?

Newsela: https://newsela.com/articles/lib-Nasa-volcano/id/23120/

Figure 7.49. A completed, modified activity using the Investigate It strategy to give the student the opportunity to explore a concept related to the grade-level Earth Science curriculum.

STRATEGIES FOR KNOWLEDGE UTILIZATION

40. Predict It

Students make predictions to find out about a topic that interests them.

Student Goals

- Activate prior knowledge.

- Make connections between prior knowledge and new learning.

- Anticipate future events.

- Learn to look for information that supports a prediction.

Directions for Teachers

1. Print a copy of the Predict It graphic organizer. (See Form 17 in Appendix B for a printable template.)

2. Prior to the activity, the teacher should model the most important process involved in predicting—the thinking process. Several prediction exercises may be needed for the student to fully understand the process. (See the reading example provided in Step 3.) Therefore, this activity may take some time to complete. In addition, demonstrating the use of the graphic can provide the student with a concrete explanation of the activity. An anchor chart of the steps involved in predicting can also be created as a visual reminder for the student.

3. Using an appropriate curriculum-related activity (such as a story), model the process of predicting before reading. For example, "The cover of this book looks interesting. I wonder what it will be about" or "There is a picture of a boy and a dog on the cover of this book. I wonder if the boy and the dog will go on an adventure." Discuss the clues that might help the reader make a prediction. Throughout the story, stop and demonstrate how a reader can check their prediction for accuracy.

4. Guide the student through a prediction activity to ensure that the student understands the process. Preselect stopping points for the student and prompt the student to think aloud about the accuracy of his or her prediction.

5. Provide the student with the Predict It graphic organizer. Have the student complete the graphic organizer independently or with support as needed.

Interventions

Work with a peer to make a prediction.

Give the student two or three prewritten predictions to choose from.

In lieu of written predictions, provide images for the student to use on the graphic organizer to represent what happened and what the student predicts will happen next.

Scribe the student's responses.

Enlarge the graphic organizer.

Extensions

Have students illustrate their prediction(s).

Have students refine or revise their prediction(s) as they work through the activity.

Remember

This activity can be used for a variety of subjects that involve content such as science and
   social studies.

This activity is suitable for all students.

Context for Student Work Sample

The work sample shown in Figure 7.50 illustrates how a seventh-grade student working
below grade level could learn content related to the grade-level curriculum. The class has
been learning about the scientific method. They have become familiar with the six steps of the
scientific method through an experiment called The Floating Egg. The student on a modified
program learns a less complex version of the scientific method that involves only two steps.
With assistance, the student completes the activity. The activity has been modified by conceptual difficulty and educational goals.

Example: Predict It

Name: Tony _____   Date: 4/12/18 _____

Activity: _Floating Egg Science Experiment_

Predict It

What happened?	What do I think will happen next?
The teacher put salt into a cup of water.	I think the egg will sink.
The teacher put sugar in the water.	I think the egg will float.

Figure 7.50. A completed, modified activity using the Predict It strategy to give the student the opportunity to explore a concept related to the grade-level science curriculum.

Appendix A

Helpful Resources

Listed here are helpful resources, including books, web sites, and audio and visual media, that you can use to learn more about topics related to inclusive education and curriculum modifications.

BOOKS

Aune, B., Burt, B., & Gennaro, P. (2010). *Behavior solutions for the inclusive classroom.* Arlington, TX: Future Horizons.

Borba, M., & Taylor-McMillan, B. (1989). *Esteem builders.* Rolling Hills Estates, CA: Jalmar Press.

Brownlie, F., & King, J. (2000). *Learning in safe schools.* Markham, Ontario, Canada: Pembroke.

Causton, J., & Theoharis, G. (2013). *The principal's handbook for leading inclusive schools.* Baltimore, MD: Paul H. Brookes Publishing Co.

Downing, J. (2010). *Academic instruction for students with moderate and severe intellectual disabilities in inclusive classrooms.* Thousand Oaks, CA: Corwin Press.

Fitzell, S. (2007). *Increasing the effectiveness of paraprofessionals and teachers working together.* Manchester, NH: Cogent Catalyst Publications.

Gross, M., & Marquez, R. H. (2012). *ParaEducate.* Lexington, KY: CreateSpace Independent Publishing Platform.

Hammeken, P. A. (2007). *The teacher's guide to inclusive education: 750 strategies for success. A guide for all educators.* Thousand Oaks, CA: Corwin Press.

Janney, R., & Snell, M. E. (2013). *Modifying schoolwork* (3rd ed.). Baltimore, MD: Paul H. Brookes Publishing Co.

Jorgensen, C. M., McSheehan, M., Sonnenmeier, R. M., & Mirenda, P. (2010). *The Beyond Access model.* Baltimore, MD: Paul H. Brookes Publishing Co.

Kluth, P., & Danaher, S. (2010). *From tutor scripts to talking sticks.* Baltimore, MD: Paul H. Brookes Publishing Co.

Kurth, J. A., & Gross, M. (2014). *The inclusion toolbox: Strategies and techniques for all teachers.* Thousand Oaks, CA: Corwin Press.

McLeskey, J., Waldron, N., Spooner, F., & Algozzine, B. (2014). *Handbook of effective inclusive schools.* New York, NY: Routledge.

Moore, S. (2016). *One without the other.* Winnipeg, Manitoba, Canada: Portage & Main Press.

Nelson, L., & Posey, A. (2013). *Design and deliver: Planning and teaching using universal design for learning.* Baltimore, MD: Paul H. Brookes Publishing Co.

Rapp, W., & Arndt, K. (2012). *Teaching everyone.* Baltimore, MD: Paul H. Brookes Publishing Co.

Sapon-Shevin, M. (1999). *Because we can change the world.* Boston, MA: Allyn & Bacon.

Villa, R., & Thousand, J. (2005). *Creating an inclusive school.* Alexandria, VA: Association for Supervision and Curriculum Development.

WEB SITES/BLOGS

ADDitude: Inside the ADHD Mind
https://www.additudemag.com

Blogsomemoore: Teaching and Empowering All Students
https://blogsomemoore.com/2013/02/

British Columbia Teachers' Federation: Teaching to Diversity
http://www.bctf.ca/Teachingtodiversity/

Brookes Inclusion Lab
http://www.brookesinclusionlab.com

Creative Mathematics
http://www.creativemathematics.com/learn/

edHelper
http://edhelper.com/

Friendship Circle: Special Needs Blog
http://www.friendshipcircle.org/blog/

Glenda's Assistive Technology
http://atclassroom.blogspot.com

Inclusive Schools Network
http://inclusiveschools.org

Kids Included Together
http://www.KIT.org

Maryland Coalition for Inclusive Education
http://www.mcie.org

Michele Borba
http://micheleborba.com

Multi-Tiered System of Supports Site-Based Intervention and Supports Guidance
http://www.sfusd.edu/en/assets/sfusd-staff/councils-and-committees/files/SSC/mtss-site-based-intervention-guidelines.pdf

National Catholic Board on Full Inclusion
http://fullinclusionforcatholicschools.org

Ollibean
http://ollibean.com

ParaEducate: Resources for Special Education
http://www.paraeducate.com

Paula Kluth
http://www.paulakluth.com

Removing the Stumbling Block
http://jewishspecialneeds.blogspot.com

Responsive Classroom
https://www.responsiveclassroom.org

SERGE (Special Education Resources for General Educators)
http://serge.ccsso.org/index.html

SET-BC (Special Education Technology: British Columbia)
https://www.setbc.org

Susan Fitzell
http://susanfitzell.com

SWIFT Schools
http://www.swiftschools.org

The Inclusive Class
http://www.theinclusiveclass.com

The Mailbox Magazine
https://www.themailbox.com/

Think Inclusive
http://www.thinkinclusive.us

Understood: For Learning and Attention Issues
https://www.understood.org/en

AUDIO/VIDEO

Including Isaac
https://youtu.be/lcPvZtt7MgE

Including Samuel
http://www.includingsamuel.com

Isn't It a Pity? The Real Problem with Special Needs
https://youtu.be/UJ7QaCFbizo

"SWIFT in 60" Films
https://vimeo.com/album/3104710

The Inclusive Class Podcast
http://inclusiveclass.libsyn.com

The Inclusive Class YouTube Channel
https://www.youtube.com/channel/UCy8NpcucwzL025anb0VtN5g

Under the Table—The Importance of Presuming Competence
https://youtu.be/AGptAXTV7m0

• •

Want to Bring Out the Best in People? Start with Strengths
https://youtu.be/MtduVS9BSxw

What Is a Multi-Tier System of Supports (MTSS)?
https://youtu.be/IjyzTNfwdCU

Who Cares About Kelsey?
http://www.whocaresaboutkelsey.com/home

Why Inclusion Works in an Educational Setting (online professional development course)
https://www.kit.org/what-we-do/online-training/inclusive-class/

APPENDIX B

· · · · · · · · · · · ·

Helpful Forms

· · · · · · · · · · · ·

Here are printable templates you can use to implement some of the strategies described in this book.

Form 1. Getting to Know Your Child

Form 2. Identify It

Form 3. Who, When, and Where Is It?

Form 4. List It

Form 5. Solving Two-Digit Addition With Regrouping

Form 6. Retell It

Form 7. Tell It With a Timeline

Form 8. I Know It. I Learned It.

Form 9. Tell Me a Story About It

Form 10. Put It in a Flowchart

Form 11. Note It

Form 12. Report It

Form 13. Chart It

Form 14. Compare It and Contrast It

Form 15. Judge It for Yourself

Form 16. Investigate It

Form 17. Predict It

Getting to Know Your Child

This information will help me teach your child this year!

Child's name (preferred name) is _____

List three to five words that describe your child's character. _____
_____

What are your child's strengths? _____
_____

What are your child's favorite activities? _____
_____

Who are your child's friends?_____

What are your child's favorite subjects in school? _____
_____

What are your child's least favorite subjects in school? _____
_____

Do you have any concerns about your child's progress in school?_____
_____

What hopes or goals do you have for your child this year?_____
_____

Do you have any other information you would like to share?

_____

_____

Thank you!

Inclusion in Action: Practical Strategies to Modify Your Curriculum by Nicole Eredics.
Copyright © 2018 by Paul H. Brookes Publishing Co., Inc. All rights reserved.

Name: _____

Date: _____

Identify It

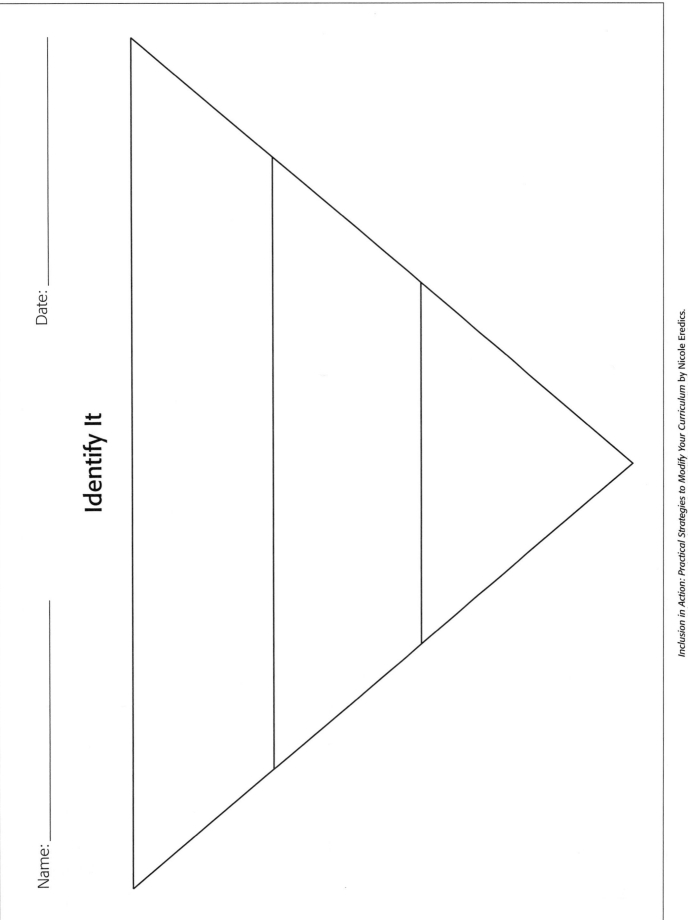

Inclusion in Action: Practical Strategies to Modify Your Curriculum by Nicole Eredics.
Copyright © 2018 by Paul H. Brookes Publishing Co., Inc. All rights reserved.

Name: _____   Date: _____

Title:_____

Who, When, and Where Is It?

WHO?

WHEN?

WHERE?

Inclusion in Action: Practical Strategies to Modify Your Curriculum by Nicole Eredics.
Copyright © 2018 by Paul H. Brookes Publishing Co., Inc. All rights reserved.

Name: _____

Date: _____

List It

Topic:		

Inclusion in Action: Practical Strategies to Modify Your Curriculum by Nicole Eredics.
Copyright © 2018 by Paul H. Brookes Publishing Co., Inc. All rights reserved.

Name: _____   Date: _____

Solving Two-Digit Addition With Regrouping

Step 1:
Copy the problem into the chart.
Line up the numbers in the correct column.

Step 2:
Add the two numbers that are in the **Ones** column.
Print the answer below.

Step 3:
Add the two numbers that are in the **Tens** column.
Print the answer below.

Tens | Ones

+

Inclusion in Action: Practical Strategies to Modify Your Curriculum by Nicole Eredics.
Copyright © 2018 by Paul H. Brookes Publishing Co., Inc. All rights reserved.

Name: _____   Date: _____

Retell It

Beginning	Middle	End

Inclusion in Action: Practical Strategies to Modify Your Curriculum by Nicole Eredics.
Copyright © 2018 by Paul H. Brookes Publishing Co., Inc. All rights reserved.

Name: _____   Date: _____

Tell It With a Timeline

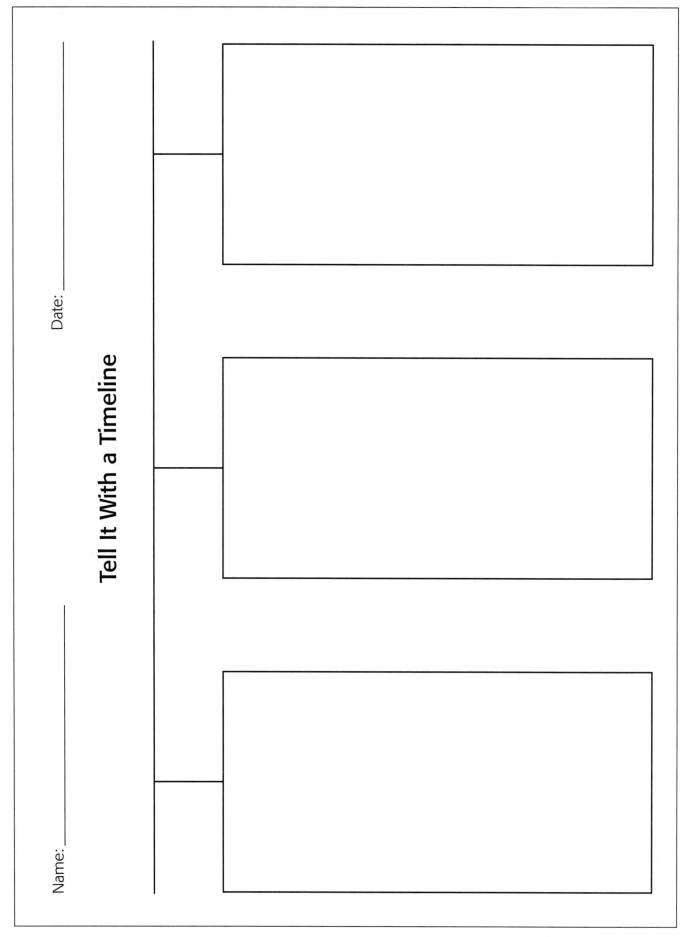

Inclusion in Action: Practical Strategies to Modify Your Curriculum by Nicole Eredics.
Copyright © 2018 by Paul H. Brookes Publishing Co., Inc. All rights reserved.

Name: _____   Date: _____

I Know It. I Learned It.

Topic: _____

I Know	I Learned

Inclusion in Action: Practical Strategies to Modify Your Curriculum by Nicole Eredics.
Copyright © 2018 by Paul H. Brookes Publishing Co., Inc. All rights reserved.

Name: _____

Date: _____

Tell Me a Story About It

First,

Then,

Finally,

Inclusion in Action: Practical Strategies to Modify Your Curriculum by Nicole Eredics.
Copyright © 2018 by Paul H. Brookes Publishing Co., Inc. All rights reserved.

Name: _____   Date: _____

Put It in a Flowchart

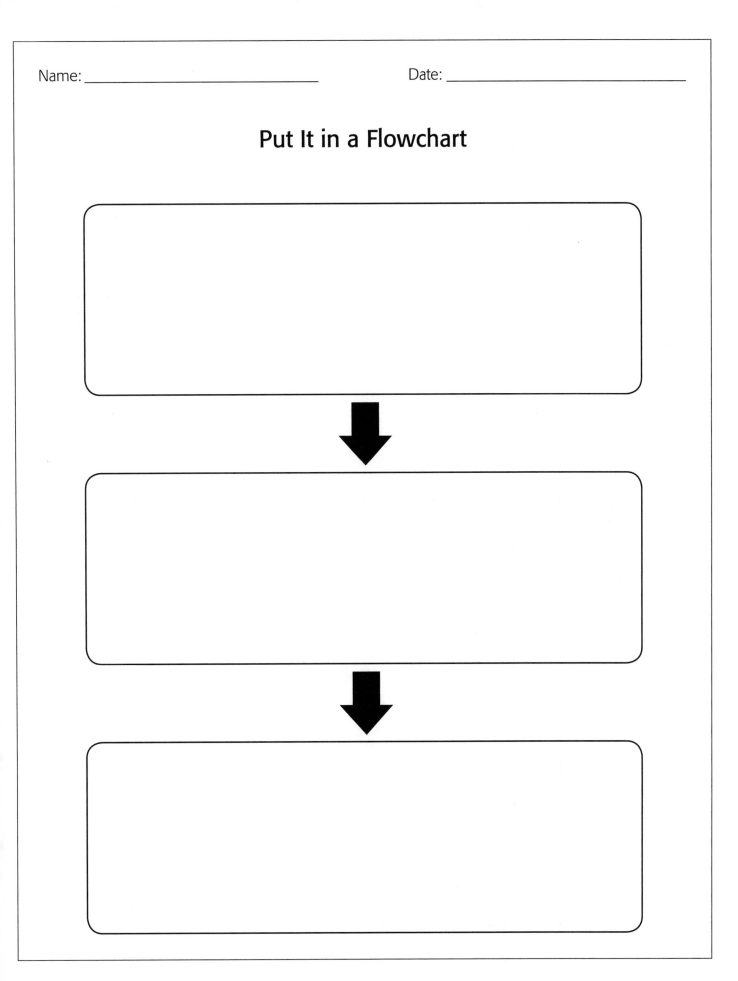

Inclusion in Action: Practical Strategies to Modify Your Curriculum by Nicole Eredics.
Copyright © 2018 by Paul H. Brookes Publishing Co., Inc. All rights reserved.

Name: _____   Date: _____

Note It

Topic	Big Ideas About the Topic

Inclusion in Action: Practical Strategies to Modify Your Curriculum by Nicole Eredics.
Copyright © 2018 by Paul H. Brookes Publishing Co., Inc. All rights reserved.

Name: _____   Date: _____

Report It

Title:

Author:

Setting:

Characters:

Beginning

Middle

End

Inclusion in Action: Practical Strategies to Modify Your Curriculum by Nicole Eredics.
Copyright © 2018 by Paul H. Brookes Publishing Co., Inc. All rights reserved.

Name: _____   Date: _____

Chart It

Inclusion in Action: Practical Strategies to Modify Your Curriculum by Nicole Eredics.
Copyright © 2018 by Paul H. Brookes Publishing Co., Inc. All rights reserved.

Name: _____

Date: _____

Compare It and Contrast It

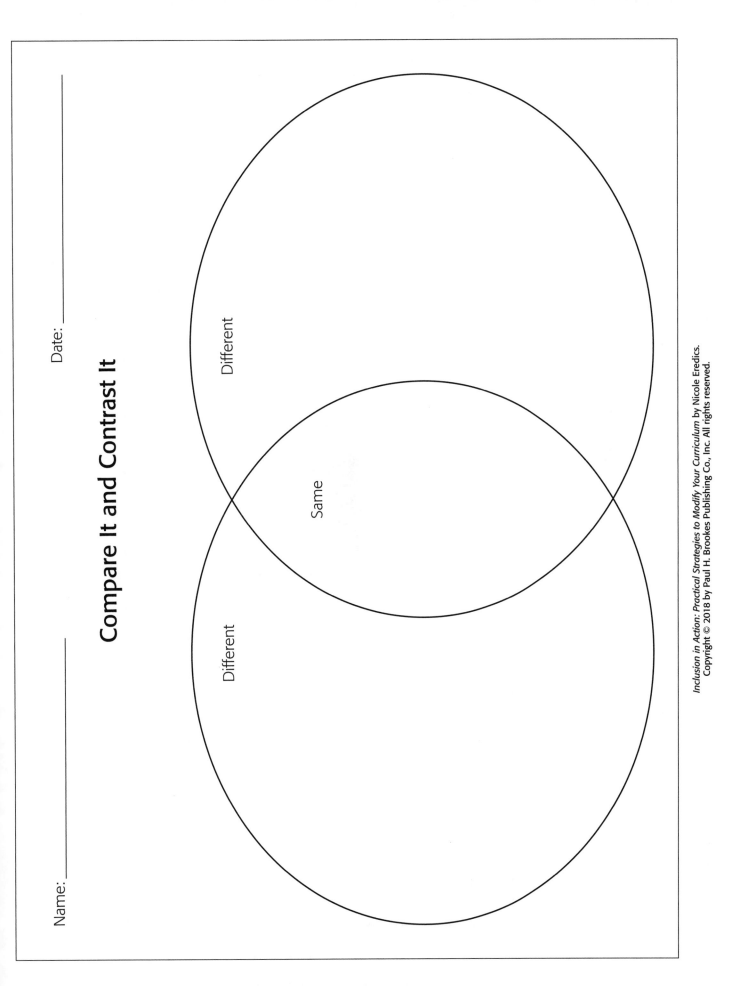

Different

Same

Different

Inclusion in Action: Practical Strategies to Modify Your Curriculum by Nicole Eredics.
Copyright © 2018 by Paul H. Brookes Publishing Co., Inc. All rights reserved.

Name: _____

Date: _____

Judge It for Yourself

What did you do?

Then what happened?

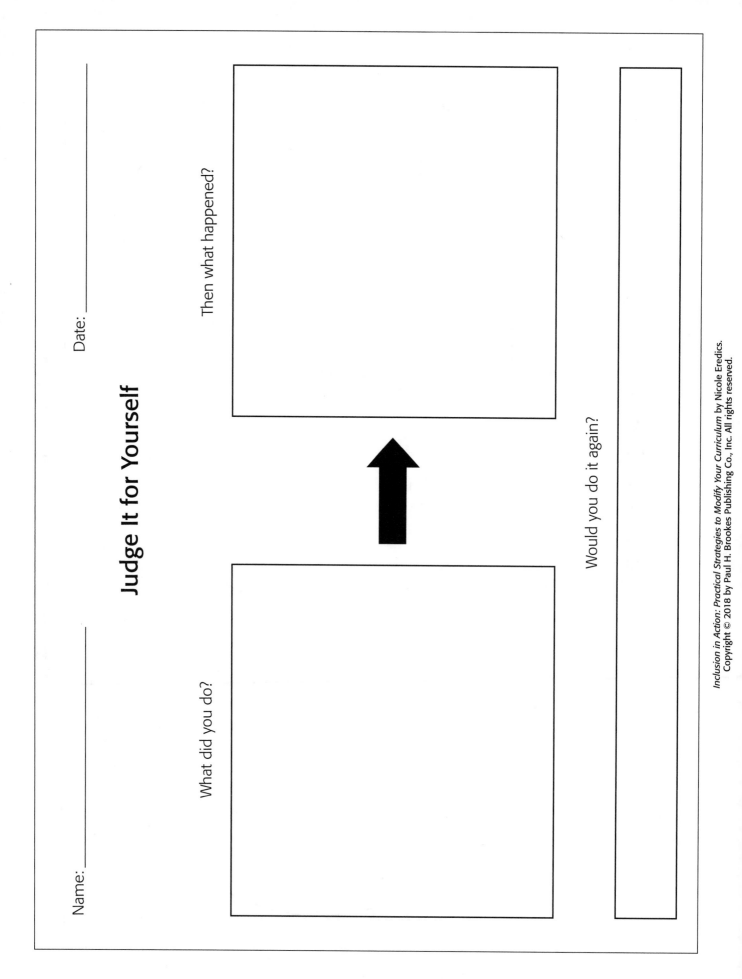

Would you do it again?

Inclusion in Action: Practical Strategies to Modify Your Curriculum by Nicole Eredics.
Copyright © 2018 by Paul H. Brookes Publishing Co., Inc. All rights reserved.

Investigate It

Topic:

Report by:

Date:

1. What is it?

2. Tell me about it.

3. Why do you like it?

4. Where did you get your information from?

Inclusion in Action: Practical Strategies to Modify Your Curriculum by Nicole Eredics.
Copyright © 2018 by Paul H. Brookes Publishing Co., Inc. All rights reserved.

Name: _____   Date: _____

Activity: _____

Predict It

What happened?	What do I think will happen next?

Inclusion in Action: Practical Strategies to Modify Your Curriculum by Nicole Eredics.
Copyright © 2018 by Paul H. Brookes Publishing Co., Inc. All rights reserved.

References

Allday, R., Neilsen-Gatti, S., & Hudson, T. (2013). Preparation for inclusion in teacher education pre-service curricula. *Teacher Education And Special Education: The Journal of The Teacher Education Division of The Council For Exceptional Children, 36*(4), 298–311. http://dx.doi.org/10.1177/0888406413497485

American Association on Intellectual and Developmental Disabilities (AAIDD). (2017). *Definition of intellectual disability: Adaptive behavior.* Retrieved from https://aaidd.org/intellectual-disability/definition#.WYTYg1Hlrcc

American Speech-Language-Hearing Association. (2015). Graduation rates rise for students with disabilities. *The ASHA Leader, 20*(6), 12. http://dx.doi.org/10.1044/leader.nib10.20062015.12

Americans with Disabilities Act (ADA) of 1990, PL 101-336, 42 U.S.C. §§ 12101 *et seq.*

Aron, L. & Loprest, P. (2012). Disability and the Education System. *The Future of Children 2*(1), 97–122.

Biklen, D., & Burke, J. (2006). Presuming competence. *Equity & Excellence in Education, 39*(2), 166–175. http://dx.doi.org/10.1080/10665680500540376

Blanton, L., Pugach, M., & Florian, L. (2011). *Preparing general education teachers to improve outcomes for students with disabilities.* Washington, DC: American Association of Colleges for Teacher Education and The National Center for Learning Disabilities.

Bloom, B. (1956). *Taxonomy of educational objectives.* New York, NY: Longmans, Green.

Brookhart, S. (2010). *How to assess higher-order thinking skills in your classroom.* Alexandria, VA: Association for Supervision & Curriculum Development.

Cameron, D., & Cook, B. (2007). Attitudes of preservice teachers enrolled in an infusion preparation program regarding planning and accommodations for included students with mental retardation. *Education and Training in Developmental Disabilities, 42*(3), 353–363.

Campbell, T., & Chastain-Bogy, C. (1996). Advantages of higher level thinking for at risk children. *Rural Educator, 18*(1), 34–37.

Carnine, D. (1991). Curricular interventions for teaching higher order thinking to all students: Introduction to the special series. *Journal of Learning Disabilities, 24*(5), 261–269. http://dx.doi.org/10.1177/002221949102400502

CAST National Center on Universal Design for Learning. (2016). *What is universal design for learning?* Retrieved from http://www.udlcenter.org/aboutudl/whatisudl

Causton, J., & Tracy-Bronson, C. P. (2015). *The educator's handbook for inclusive school practices.* Baltimore, MD: Paul H. Brookes Publishing Co.

Center on Education Policy. (2007). *Why we still need public schools: Public education for the common good.* Washington, DC: Author.

Classroom Management. (2014, November 26). In S. Abbott (Ed.), *The glossary of education reform.* Retrieved from http://edglossary.org/classroom-management/

Cole, C., Waldron, N., & Majd, M. (2004). Academic progress of students across inclusive and traditional settings. *Mental Retardation, 42*(2), 136–144. http://dx.doi.org/10.1352/0047-6765(2004)42<136:aposai>2.0.co;2

Collaborative for Academic, Social, and Emotional Learning (CASEL). (2017). *CASEL program guides. Effective social and emotional learning programs.* Retrieved from http://www.casel.org/guide/

Common Core State Standards Initiative. (n.d.). *Application for students with disabilities.* Retrieved from http://www.corestandards.org/wp-content/uploads/Application-to-Students-with-Disabilities-again-for-merge.pdf

Cook-Harvey, C. M., Darling-Hammond, L., Lam, L., Mercer, C., & Roc, M. (2016). Equity and ESSA: Leveraging educational opportunity through the Every Student Succeeds Act. Palo Alto, CA: Learning Policy Institute. Retrieved from http://learningpolicyinstitute.org/product/equity-essa

Covey, S., & Covey, S. (2014). *The leader in me: How schools around the world are inspiring greatness, one child at a time.* New York, NY: Simon & Schuster.

Cowen, C. (2016). Dyslexia and visuospatial processing strengths: New research sheds light. *The Center for Development and Learning.* Retrieved from http://www.cdl.org/articles/dyslexia-and-visuospatial-processing-strengths-%E2%80%A8new-research-sheds-light/

Deno, E. (1970). Special education as developmental capital. *Exceptional Children, 37,* 229–237.

Dessemontet, R., Bless, G., & Morin, D. (2011). Effects of inclusion on the academic achievement and adaptive behaviour of children with intellectual disabilities. *Journal of Intellectual Disability Research, 56*(6), 579–587. http://dx.doi.org/10.1111/j.1365-2788.2011.01497.x

Donovan, S., & Cross, C. (2002). *Minority students in special and gifted education.* Washington, DC: National Academy Press.

Doran, G. T. (1981). There's a S.M.A.R.T. way to write management's goals and objectives. *Management Review, 70*(11), 35–36.

Dunn, L. (1968). Special education for the mildly retarded—Is much of it justifiable? *Exceptional Children, 35,* 5–22.

Durham District School Board: Equity and Inclusive Education Working Group. (2009). *Guidelines for inclusive language.* Durham, Ontario, Canada. Retrieved from http://www.ddsb.ca/AboutUs/Equity InclusiveEducation/Documents/Guidelines_ Inclusive_Language.pdf

Durlak, J., Weissberg, R., Dymnicki, A., Taylor, R., & Schellinger, K. (2011). The impact of enhancing students' social and emotional learning: A meta-analysis of school-based universal interventions. *Child Development, 82*(1), 405–432. http://dx.doi.org/10.1111/j.1467-8624.2010.01564.x

Elias, M. J., Zins, J. E., Weissberg, R. P., Frey, K. S., Greenberg, M. T., Haynes, N. M., . . ., Shriver, T. P. (1997). *Promoting social and emotional learning: Guidelines for educators.* Alexandria, VA: Association for Supervision & Curriculum Development.

Endow, J. (2013). Autistics can BE friends. *Judy Endow: Aspects of autism translated.* Retrieved from http://www.judyendow.com/advocacy/autistics-can-be-friends/

Ermeling, B., Hiebert, J., & Gallimore, R. (2015, December 7). Beyond growth mindset: Creating classroom opportunities for meaningful struggle. Retrieved from http://www.edweek.org/tm/articles/2015/12/07/beyond-growth-mindset-creating-classroom-opportunities-for.html

Falvey, M. (2004). Toward realizing the influence of "Toward Realization of the Least Restrictive Educational Environments for Severely Handicapped Students." *Research and Practice for Persons with Severe Disabilities, 29*(1), 9–10. http://dx.doi.org/10.2511/rpsd.29.1.9

Florian, L. (2005). "Inclusion," "special needs" and the search for new understandings. *Support for Learning, 20*(2), 96–98. http://dx.doi.org/10.1111/j.0268-2141.2005.00368.x

Forest, M., & Pearpoint, J. (1995). The criteria for being included: Breathing (with a respirator if you need one!). *Inclusion Network: Training tools.* Retrieved from http://www.inclusion.com/ttcriteria.html

Forlin, C., Loreman, T., Sharma, U., & Earle, C. (2009). Demographic differences in changing preservice teachers' attitudes, sentiments and concerns about inclusive education. *International Journal of Inclusive Education, 13*(2), 195–209. http://dx.doi.org/10.1080/13603110701365356

Frey, K., Hirschstein, M., Snell, J., Edstrom, L., MacKenzie, E., & Broderick, C. (2005). Reducing playground bullying and supporting beliefs: An experimental trial of the Steps to Respect Program. *Developmental Psychology, 41*(3), 479–490. http://dx.doi.org/10.1037/0012-1649.41.3.479

Friend, M., Cook, L., Hurley-Chamberlain, D., & Shamberger, C. (2010). Co-teaching: An illustration of the complexity of collaboration in special education. *Journal of Educational and Psychological Consultation, 20*(1), 9–27. http://dx.doi.org/10.1080/10474410903535380

Gabriel, J., & Farmer, P. (2009). *How to help your school thrive without breaking the bank.* Alexandria, VA: Association for Supervision and Curriculum Development.

Geschwind, N. (1982). Why Orton was right. *Annals of Dyslexia, 32*(1), 13–30. http://dx.doi.org/10.1007/bf02647951

Gibbs, J. (2016). *Reaching all by creating tribes learning communities.* Coverdale, CA: Center Source Systems.

Goodenow, C. (1993). The psychological sense of school membership among adolescents: Scale development and educational correlates. *Psychology in the Schools, 30*(1), 79–90. http://dx.doi.org/10.1002/1520-6807(199301)30:1<79::aid-pits2310300113>3.0.co;2-x

Gordon, M. (2009) *Roots of empathy: Changing the world child by child.* New York, NY: Experiment Publishing.

Gray, C. (2010). *The new social story book.* Arlington, TX: Future Horizons.

Grima-Farrell, C., Bain, A., & McDonagh, S. (2011). Bridging the research-to-practice gap: A review of the literature focusing on inclusive education. *Australasian Journal of Special Education, 35*(2), 117–136. http://dx.doi.org/10.1375/ajse.35.2.117

Hall, J. (1996). Integration, inclusion: What does it all mean? In J. Coupe & J. Goldbart (Eds.), *Whose choice? Contentious issues for those working with people with learning difficulties.* London, England: David Fulton.

Hall, T., Vue, G., Koga, N., & Silva, S. (2004). *Curriculum modification.* Wakefield, MA: National Center on Accessing the General Curriculum.

Heller, K., Holtzman, W., & Messick, S. (Eds.). (1982). *Placing children in special education: A strategy for equity.* Washington, DC: National Academy Press.

Individuals with Disabilities Education Improvement Act (IDEA) of 2004, PL 108-446, 20 U.S.C. §§ 1400 *et seq.*

Jalloul, F. & EL-Daou, B. (2016). The effect of training individuals with mild intellectual disability in scaffolding strategies and computer software on their generalization skills. *World Journal on Educational Technology: Current Issues, 8*(3), 277–293.

Janney, R., & Snell, M. E. (2013). *Modifying schoolwork* (3rd ed.). Baltimore, MD: Paul H. Brookes Publishing Co.

Jeynes, W. H. (2005). A meta-analysis of the relation of parental involvement to urban elementary school student academic achievement. *Urban Education, 40*(3), 237–269.

Jones, D., Greenberg, M., & Crowley, M. (2015a). Early social-emotional functioning and public health: The relationship between kindergarten social competence and future wellness. *American Journal of Public Health, 105*(11), 2283–2290. http://dx.doi.org/10.2105/ajph.2015.302630

Jones, D., Greenberg, M., & Crowley, M. (2015b). *How children's social skills impact success in adulthood.* Princeton, NJ: Robert Wood Johnson Foundation.

Jorgensen, C., McSheehan, M., & Sonnenmeier, R. (2007). Presumed competence reflected in the educational programs of students with IDD before and after the Beyond Access professional development intervention. *Journal of Intellectual and Developmental Disability, 32*(4), 248–262. http://dx.doi.org/10.1080/13668250701704238

Kalambouka, A., Farrell, P., Dyson, A., & Kaplan, I. (2007). The impact of placing pupils with special educational needs in mainstream schools on the achievement of their peers. *Educational Research, 49*(4), 365–382. http://dx.doi.org/10.1080/00131880701717222

Katz, J., & Porath, M. (2011). Teaching to diversity: Creating compassionate learning communities for diverse elementary school students. *International Journal of Special Education, 26*(2), 29–41.

Kessler Foundation. (2017). nTIDE 2016 year-end special report: Upward momentum fuels positive start to 2017 for Americans with disabilities. Retrieved from https://kesslerfoundation.org/content/ntide-2016-year-end-special-report-upward-momentum-fuels-positive-start-2017-americans

Kunsch, C., Jitendra, A., & Sood, S. (2007). The effects of peer-mediated instruction in mathematics for students with learning problems: A research synthesis. *Learning Disabilities Research & Practice, 22*(1), 1–12. http://dx.doi.org/10.1111/j.1540-5826.2007.00226.x

Kurth, J., Morningstar, M., & Kozleski, E. (2014). The persistence of highly restrictive special education placements for students with low-incidence disabilities. *Research and Practice for Persons With Severe Disabilities, 39*(3), 227–239. http://dx.doi.org/10.1177/1540796914555580

Lee, S. H., Wehmeyer, M. L., Soukup, J. H., & Palmer, S. B. (2010). Impact of curriculum modifications on access to the general education curriculum for students with disabilities. *Exceptional Children. 76*(2), 213–233.

Lombardi, T., & Savage, L. (1994). Higher order thinking skills for students with special needs. *Preventing School Failure: Alternative Education for Children and Youth, 38*(4), 27–31. http://dx.doi.org/10.1080/1045988x.1994.9944318

Lopez, S., & Louis, M. (2009). The principles of strengths-based education. *Journal of College and Character, 10*(4). http://dx.doi.org/10.2202/1940-1639.1041

Loreman, T., Forlin, C., Chambers, D., Sharma, U., & Deppeler, J. (2014). Conceptualising and measuring inclusive education. In T. Loreman & C. Forlin (Eds.), *Measuring inclusive education* (p. 6). Bingley, England: Emerald Group Publishing.

Marzano, R. J., & Kendall, J. S. (2007). *The new taxonomy of educational objectives.* Thousand Oaks, CA: Corwin Press.

Marzano, R. J., & Kendall, J. S. (2008). *Designing and assessing educational objectives: Applying the new taxonomy.* Thousand Oaks, CA: Corwin Press.

Maslow, A. (1962). *Toward a psychology of being.* Princeton, NJ: Van Nostrand.

McDonnell, J., Thorson, N., Disher, S., Mathot-Buckner, C., Mendel, J., & Ray, L. (2003). The achievement of students with developmental disabilities and their peers without disabilities in inclusive settings: An exploratory study. *Education and Treatment of Children, 26*(3), 224–236.

McGregor, G., & Vogelsberg, R. (1998). *Inclusive schooling practices: Pedagogical and research foundations. A synthesis of the literature that informs best practices about inclusive schooling.* Pittsburgh, PA: Allegheny University of the Health Sciences.

McNulty, R., & Gloeckler, L. (2014). *Fewer, clearer, higher Common Core State Standards: Implications for students receiving special education services.* International Center for Leadership in Education. Retrieved from http://www.leadered.com/pdf/fewer_clearer_higher_ccss_special_education_2014.pdf

Means, B., & Knapp, M. (1991). Cognitive approaches to teaching advanced skills to educationally disadvantaged students. *The Phi Delta Kappan, 73*(4), 282–289.

Meston, L., & Cranston, R. (2011). Making adaptations and modifications to improve learning. In F. Brownlie & J. King (Eds.), *Learning in safe schools* (2nd ed., p. 80). Markham, Ontario, Canada: Pembroke Publishers.

Morgan, P. (2006). Increasing task engagement using preference or choice-making: Some behavioral and methodological factors affecting their efficacy as classroom interventions. *Remedial and Special Education, 27*(3), 176–187. http://dx.doi.org/10.1177/07419325060270030601

National Center for Education Statistics. (2016). Children and youth with disabilities [indicator]. From *The Condition of Education: Participation in Education; Elementary/Secondary Enrollment.* Retrieved from http://nces.ed.gov/programs/coe/indicator_cgg.asp

National Collaborative on Workforce and Disability. (2017). *Attitudinal barriers for people with disabilities.* Retrieved from http://www.ncwd-youth.info/attitudinal-barriers-for-people-with-disabilities

National Governors Association Center for Best Practices and the Council of Chief State School Officers. (2010). Application to students with disabilities (pp. 1–2). From *Common Core State Standards Initiative.* Washington, DC: Author.

National Governors Association Center for Best Practices and the Council of Chief State School Officers. (2017). About the standards. *Common Core State Standards Initiative.* Retrieved from http://www.corestandards.org/about-the-standards/

National Research Council. (1987). *Education and learning to think*. Washington, DC: National Academies Press. https://doi.org/10.17226/1032

Newcomb, A., Bukowski, W., & Pattee, L. (1993). Children's peer relations: A meta-analytic review of popular, rejected, neglected, controversial, and average sociometric status. *Psychological Bulletin, 113*(1), 99–128. http://dx.doi.org/10.1037/0033-2909.113.1.99

Ogle, D. M. (1986). K-W-L: A teaching model that develops active reading of expository text. *Reading Teacher, 39,* 564–570.

Okilwa, N. S. A., & Shelby, L. (2010). The effects of peer tutoring on academic performance of students with disabilities in grades 6 through 12: A synthesis of the literature. *Remedial and Special Education, 31*(6), 450–463. Retrieved from http://journals.sagepub.com/doi/abs/10.1177/0741932509355991

Osgood, R. (2005). *The history of inclusion in the United States.* Washington, DC: Gallaudet University Press.

Osterman, K. (2000). Students' need for belonging in the school community. *Review of Educational Research, 70*(3), 323–367. http://dx.doi.org/10.3102/00346543070003323

Piaget, J. (1960). *The psychology of intelligence.* Garden City, NY: Littlefield, Adams & Co.

Province of British Columbia. (2016). *Special education: Policy statement.* Retrieved from http://www2.gov.bc.ca/gov/content/education-training/administration/legislation-policy/public-schools/special-education

Ralabate, P. K. (2016). *Your UDL lesson planner: the step-by-step guide for teaching all learners.* Baltimore, MD: Paul H. Brookes Publishing Co.

Rehabilitation Act of 1973, PL 93-112, 29 U.S.C. §§ 701 et seq.

Reynolds, M. (1962). A framework for considering some issues in special education. *Exceptional Children, 28*(7), 367–370.

Reynolds, M., & Birch, J. (1982). *Teaching exceptional children in all America's schools.* Reston, VA: Council for Exceptional Children.

Riehl, C. (2000). The principal's role in creating inclusive schools for diverse students: A review of normative, empirical, and critical literature on the practice of educational administration. *Review of Educational Research, 70*(1), 55. http://dx.doi.org/10.2307/1170594

Rothwell, J. (1981). *Telling it like it isn't.* Englewood Cliffs, NJ: Prentice Hall.

Salisbury, C., Mangino, M., Petrigala, M., Rainforth, B., Syryca, S., & Palombaro, M. (1994). Promoting the instructional inclusion of young children with disabilities in the primary grades. *Journal of Early Intervention, 18*(3), 311–322. http://dx.doi.org/10.1177/105381519401800306

Shapiro, E. (n.d.). Tiered instruction and intervention in a response-to-intervention model. *RTI Action Network: A Program of the National Center for Learning Disabilities.* Retrieved from http://rtinetwork.org/essential/tieredinstruction/tiered-instruction-and-intervention-rti-model

Sharma, U., & Nuttal, A. (2015). The impact of training on pre-service teacher attitudes, concerns, and efficacy towards inclusion. *Asia-Pacific Journal of Teacher Education, 44*(2), 142–155. http://dx.doi.org/10.1080/1359866x.2015.1081672

Sharpe, M., York, J., & Knight, J. (1994). Effects of inclusion on the academic performance of classmates without disabilities: A preliminary study. *Remedial and Special Education, 15*(5), 281–287. http://dx.doi.org/10.1177/074193259401500503

Soodak, L. (2003). Classroom management in inclusive settings. *Theory Into Practice, 42*(4), 327–333. http://dx.doi.org/10.1353/tip.2003.0050

Switlick, D. (1997). Curriculum modifications and adaptations. In D. Bradley, M. King-Sears, & D. Switlick (Eds.), *Teaching students in inclusive settings* (p. 236). Needham Heights, MA: Allyn & Bacon.

Taylor, G., & MacKenney, L. (2008). *Improving human learning in the classroom: Theories and teaching practices.* Lanham, MD: Rowman & Littlefield Education.

Taylor, S. (1988). Caught in the continuum: A critical analysis of the principle of the least restrictive environment. *Research and Practice for Persons With Severe Disabilities, 13*(1), 41–53. http://dx.doi.org/10.1177/154079698801300105

The Arc. (2016). *What is people first language?* Retrieved from http://www.thearc.org/who-we-are/media-center/people-first-language

Theoharis, G., & Causton-Theoharis, J. (2016). *Educational leadership: Interventions that work—Include, belong, learn.* Association for Supervision and Curriculum Development. Retrieved from http://www.ascd.org/publications/educational-leadership/oct10/vol68/num02/Include,-Belong,-Learn.aspx

United Nations Educational, Scientific, and Cultural Organization. (1994). *The Salamanca statement and framework for action on special needs education.* Salamanca, Spain: Author. Retrieved from http://www.unesco.org/education/pdf/SALAMA_E.PDF

United Nations Educational, Scientific, and Cultural Organization (Bangkok office). (2016). *Barriers to inclusive education.* Retrieved from http://www.unescobkk.org/education/inclusive-education/what-is-inclusive-education/barriers-to-inclusive-education/

United States Department of Education. (2016). *Building the legacy: IDEA 2004.* Retrieved from http://idea.ed.gov/

United States Government Accountability Office. (2009). *Multiple federal education offices support teacher preparation for instructing students with disabilities and English language learners, but systematic department-wide coordination could enhance this assistance* (GAO-09-573). Washington, DC: Government Accountability Office.

Vygotsky, L. S. (1978). *Mind in society: The development of higher psychological processes.* M. Cole, V. John-Steiner, S. Scribner, & E. Souberman (Eds.). Cambridge, MA: Harvard University Press.

Warshauer, H. K. (2014). Productive struggle in middle school mathematics classrooms. *Journal of Mathematics Teacher Education, 18*(4), 375–400. http://dx.doi.org/10.1007/s10857-014-9286-3

Weller, D., & McLeskey, J. (2000). Block scheduling and inclusion in a high school. *Remedial and Special Education, 21*(4), 209–218. http://dx.doi.org/10.1177/074193250002100402

Wenglinsky, H. (2001, September). *Teacher classroom practices and student performance: How schools can make a difference.* Princeton, NJ: Educational Testing Service. Retrieved from https://www.ets.org/Media/Research/pdf/RR-01-19-Wenglinsky.pdf

Whitworth, J. (1999). A model for inclusive teacher preparation. *Electronic Journal of Inclusive Education, 1*(2), 1–8.

Wiener, J., & Tardif, C. (2004). Social and emotional functioning of children with learning disabilities: Does special education placement make a difference? *Learning Disabilities Research and Practice, 19*(1), 20–32. http://dx.doi.org/10.1111/j.1540-5826.2004.00086.x

Will, M. (1986). Educating children with learning problems: A shared responsibility. *Exceptional Children, 52*(5), 411–415.

Wilson, C. H., Ellerbee, K. L., & Christian, S. H. (2011, April). Best practices of inclusion at the elementary level. Retrieved from http://files.eric.ed.gov/fulltext/ED522452.pdf

Yudin, M. K., & Musgrove, M. (2015). *Guidance on FAPE.* Retrieved from https://www2.ed.gov/policy/speced/guid/idea/memosdcltrs/guidance-on-fape-11-17-2015.pdf

Zigmond, N., & Magiera, K. (2001). A focus on co-teaching. Use with caution. *Current Practice Alerts, 6*, 1–4. Retrieved from http://TeachingLD.org/alerts

Zohar, A., & Dori, Y. (2003). Higher order thinking skills and low-achieving students: Are they mutually exclusive? *Journal of the Learning Sciences, 12*(2), 145–181. http://dx.doi.org/10.1207/s15327809jls1202_1

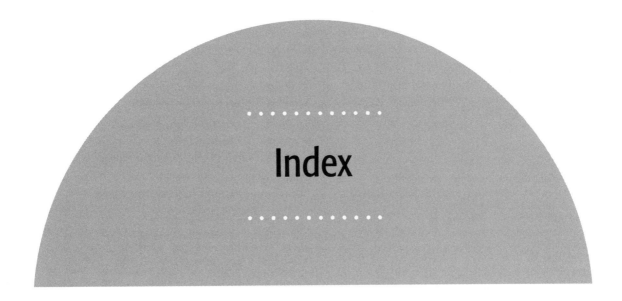

Index

References to tables and figures are indicated with a *t* and *f*, respectively.

Academic benefits of inclusion, 11–12
Accommodations, 39
Adaptive behavior, 65
Administrators, 13–14
Altering conceptual difficulty, in curriculum
    modification, 47
Altering content, in curriculum modification, 47
Altering educational goals, in curriculum
    modification, 47
Altering the instructional method, in curriculum
    modification, 47
Alternate teaching, 25
American Association on Intellectual and
    Developmental Disabilities (AAIDD), 65
Americans with Disabilities Act (ADA) of 1990, 43
Analysis strategies, 61
Assign classroom jobs, 31
Assistive communication device, 8, 8*f*

Big buddy system, 32
Blatt, Burton, 4
Bloom's taxonomy, 60
Bus drivers, 15

Cascade model of services, 5
Chart It strategy, 136–137, 137*f*, 172*f*
Choose It strategy, 105–106, 106*f*
Class meetings, 32
Classroom, 21*t*
    co-teacher, 25
    families, 26–27
    inclusive, 23–29
    paraprofessional, 26, 28*t*
    peers, 28–29, 29*f*
    strength-based, 29–30
    teacher, 24
    volunteers, 28

Classroom culture, 29–34
Classroom management style, 32–33
Clear and manageable tasks, 33–34
Cloze It strategy, 122–123, 123*f*
Co-teacher, 25
Collaborative teaching opportunities, 24
Collect It strategy, 134, 135*f*
Common Core State Standards (CCSS), 58
Compare and Contrast It strategy, 140–141, 141*f*, 173*f*
Comprehension strategies, 61
Conceptual difficulty, in curriculum modification, 47
Conceptual skills, 65
Copy It strategy, 97, 98*f*
Counselors, 14
Cross It Out strategy, 72, 73*f*
Curriculum
    accessibility, 37–44, 46
    accommodations, 43–44
Curriculum modifications, 44, 45–54
    altering conceptual difficulty, 47
    altering content, 47
    altering educational goals, 47
    altering the instructional method, 47
    basics of, 46–47
    how they are made, 50–51
    instructional strategies, 59–61
    language arts, 49*f*
    maintaining high standards, 58
    purpose of, 48–49
    research-based, 57–62
    resources to learn more, 155–157
    science, 48*f*
    students below grade level, 55–62
Custodians, 15
Cut It Out strategy, 118, 119*f*

Daily activities schedule, 34
Deno, Elizabeth, 5

Differentiated instruction, 24
Difficulty with applying knowledge, 66
Difficulty with comprehension skills, 66
Draw It strategy, 120, 121*f*
Dunn, Lloyd, 5

Edit It strategy, 144, 145*f*
Educational goals, in curriculum modification, 47
Educator's Handbook for Inclusive School Practices
    (Causton & Tracy-Bronson), 26
Embedded skill development, 46
Emotional benefits of inclusion, 10
Events, 19
Exclusion, 8–9, 8*f*
Executive function skill acquisition, 34

Families, 27
Feeling of belonging, 10
Find It strategy, 70, 71*f*
Follow It strategy, 101–102. 102*f*
Forest, Marsha, 9
Free appropriate public education (FAPE), 5
Front office, 21*t*

Gender-specific phrases, 18
Getting to know your child form, 160
Group It strategy, 142, 143*f*
Guidelines for Inclusive Language Policy (2009), 18

Higher order thinking skills, 60
Highlight It strategy, 83–84, 85*f*

I Know It. I Learned It. strategy, 115–116, 117*f*, 167*f*
Identify It strategy, 76, 77*f*, 161*f*
IDs, *see* Intellectual disabilities (IDs)
Inclusion, 8–9, 8*f*
Inclusion levels, 53*f*
Inclusive classroom, 23–29, 39–44
    accommodations, 43
    creating a culture, 29–34
    infrastructure, 33
    positive management style, 32–33
    reflect and response to student needs, 34–35
    setting up the space, 38–39
    social-emotional development in, 30–32, 30*f*
    techniques and strategies for teaching, 24
Inclusive education
    benefits of, 10–12
    committing to, 3–4
    core beliefs, 6–10
    educate every child, 17
    history of, 4–6
    instructional strategies and
        accommodations, 37–44
    leadership and staff roles, 13–16
    resources to learn more, 155–157
    school spaces, 20, 21*t*
    support for, 23–35

Individualized education program (IEP), 23, 43
    Program-at-a-Glance, 51*f*, 52*f*
    steps to create with curriculum
        modifications, 50–51
Individuals with Disabilities Education Improvement
    Act (IDEA) of 2004, 5
Instructional method, in curriculum modification, 47
Intake meetings, 26
Integration, 8–9, 8*f*
Intellectual disabilities (IDs), 4, 63–66
Intellectual functioning, 65
Interest inventory form, 26, 28*f*
Investigate It strategy, 148–149, 150*f*, 175*f*
Is It Yes or No? strategy, 68–69, 69*f*
It's a Letter Clue strategy, 89–90, 90*f*
It's a Number Clue strategy, 93, 94*f*

Judge It for Yourself strategy, 146–147, 147*f*, 174*f*

Knowledge utilization strategies, 61

Label It strategy, 80–81, 82*f*
Language, 18
    meaningful, respectful, and positive, 34
Large- and small-group experiences, 31–32
Leadership and staff, 13–16
Library, 21*t*
Life beyond school, beliefs about, 9–10
Limited working memory abilities, 66
List It strategy, 95–96, 96*f*, 163*f*
Lower level skills, 60
Lunch supervisors, 15

Mainstreaming, 8–9, 8*f*
Make It strategy, 113–114, 114*f*
Match It strategy, 138, 139*f*
Mission statements, 17, 17*f*
Model manners, 31
Modifications
    definition, 44
    making curriculum achievable, 45–54
Modified science activity, IEP, 52*f*
Modifying curriculum, 46
Multi-tiered system of support (MTSS), 39, 41, 42*f*
Multiple means of action and expression, in UDL, 40
Multiple means of engagement, in UDL, 40
Multiple means of representation, in UDL, 40

National Collaborative on Workforce and
    Disability, 2017, 9
Note It strategy, 128–129, 129*f*, 170*f*

Occupational therapists, 14
Office personnel, 15
One teach/one assist model of teaching, 25
One teach/one observe model of teaching, 25
One-to-one instruction, 34, 46

Parallel teaching, 25
Paraprofessional, 26, 28*t*
Pearpoint, Jack, 9
Peers, 28–29, 29*f*
    relationships, development of, 34
Pen pal program, 31
People-first language, 18
Physical environment, change in, 34
Playground, 21*t*
Positive behavior support (PBS), 34
Positive behavioral interventions and supports
    (PBIS), 34
Practical skills, 65
Predict It strategy, 151–152, 153*f*, 176*f*
Productive struggle, 59
Program-at-a-Glance, 51*f*
Prosocial skills, 10–11
Put It in a Flowchart strategy, 126–127, 127*f*, 169*f*

Read It strategy, 109–110, 110*f*
Recess supervisors, 15
Rehabilitation Act of 1973, 43
Report It strategy, 130–131, 131*f*, 171*f*
Response to intervention (RTI), 41
Retell It strategy, 103–104, 104*f*, 165*f*
Retrieval strategies, 61
Reynolds, Maynard, 5
Role-play, 31
Routines for students, 33

Schedules, 18–19
School
    accommodations, 43
    core beliefs about, 7–8
School community, 19–20
School culture, 16–19, 16*f*
School spaces, 20, 21*t*
Segregation, moving to inclusion, 4–6
Sequence It strategy, 111–112, 112*f*
Show It strategy, 99–100, 100*f*
SMART goals, 50
Social benefits of inclusion, 10–11, 11*f*
Social-emotional development, 30–32, 30*f*
Social skills, 65
Solving two-digit addition with regrouping, 164*f*
*Some Persistently Recurring Assumptions Concerning
    the Mentally Subnormal* (Blatt), 4
Specialized support staff, 14–16
Speech-language pathologists (SLPs), 14
Spell It strategy, 86–87, 88*f*
Station teaching, 25

Stories that teach social skills, 32
Strategies, 63–154, *see also* specific strategy from
    Marzano's taxonomy
    analysis, 61
    comprehension, 61
    extend thinking, 60
    forms for, 159–176
    how to use, 62
    knowledge utilization, 61
    productive struggle, 59
    retrieval, 61
    who benefits, 63–65
Strength-based classroom, 29–30
Student behavior, expectations for, 33
Students
    accommodations, 44
    core beliefs about, 6–7, 7*f*
    needs of, 34–35
Substitute It strategy, 74, 75*f*

Taylor, Steve, 5
Teacher, 24
Teaching practice and multiple experiences, 24
Team teaching, 25
Tell It with a Timeline strategy, 107–108, 108*f*, 166*f*
Tell Me a Story About It strategy, 124, 125*f*, 168*f*
*Telling it Liken It Isn't: Language Misuse and
    Malpractice* (Rothwell), 18
The New Taxonomy of Educational Objectives
    (Marzano & Kendall), 60–61, 61*f*
Toward a Psychology of Being (Maslow), 10
Trouble analyzing information, 66

United Nations Educational, Scientific, and Cultural
    Organization (UNESCO), 5–6
Universal design for learning (UDL), 24, 39–40
Use It in a Sentence strategy, 91–92, 92*f*

Volunteers, 28

Web It strategy, 132–133, 133*f*
Who, When, and Where is It? strategy, 78, 79*f*, 162*f*
*Why We Still Need Public Schools: Public Education
    for the Common Good* (Center on Education
    Policy, 2007), 9
Will, Madeline, 5

Zone of proximal development, 49